Blackboard

Also by Lewis Buzbee

Blackboard

A Personal History of the Classroom

Lewis Buzbee

GRAYWOLF PRESS

This publication is made possible, in part, by the voters of Minnesota through a Minnesota State Arts Board Operating Support grant, thanks to a legislative appropriation from the arts and cultural heritage fund, and through a grant from the Wells Fargo Foundation Minnesota. Significant support has also been provided by Target, the McKnight Foundation, Amazon.com, and other generous contributions from foundations, corporations, and individuals. To these organizations and individuals we offer our heartfelt thanks.

Published by Graywolf Press
250 Third Avenue North, Suite 600
Minneapolis, Minnesota 55401

www.graywolfpress.org

Published in the United States of America

ISBN 978-1-55597-683-5

2 4 6 8 9 7 5 3 1
First Graywolf Printing, 2014

Library of Congress Control Number: 2013958015

Cover design: Kyle G. Hunter

Cover photos: Vintage school desk © ideabug, istockphoto.com; blank blackboard © Timur Arbaev, veer.com

for every single one of
my teachers

I never wanted school to be over. I'd spend
as much time inside school as I could, poring
over books we were given, being around the
teachers, breathing in the school odors, which
were the same everywhere and like no other.
Knowing things became important to me, no
matter what they were.

—Richard Ford, *Canada*

A teacher of the best sort, whose passion had
always been—and remained—to inspire the
young into useful lives free from the tyrannies
of ignorance, and ready always to follow any
fact whithersoever it might lead.

—Doris Lessing, *Shikasta*

Contents

Blackboard

I
Orientation

Bake Sale

I've had many opportunities to stop by Bagby Elementary, but, preferring instead drive-by washes of memory, it's been decades since I've set foot here. Today, however, after lunch at her grandmother's, my daughter, Maddy, calls out from the backseat that she wants to take a closer look at my old school. Why not? she says.

It's a deep Indian summer Saturday, warm under a thin plane of rooster tail clouds sliding in from the west. The light of the shortening afternoon is golden and purple at once, and scarlet liquidambar leaves blanket the neighborhood's orderly grid of lawns and sidewalks. This is ideal back-to-school weather, at least to me. Here in the Santa Clara Valley, fifty miles south of San Francisco, the first rains have not yet returned after the bone-dry summer, and the scented air—a sharp, nearly acrid decay—tells me that school is back in session.

As a child I was at best an average student, never an overachiever, and most Septembers the loss of summer's broad freedoms seemed an incomprehensible punishment, but even so, the lure of school's return never failed to send a thrill through me. Whether I was drawn by the crush of the schoolyard and all the other kids who would be there, or unknowingly craved the structure of classes and relief from seemingly infinite summer, or simply recognized the fitness of the world's turning through time and space, no matter how loud I grumbled, the return to school was momentous.

The first day of school was a simple but ritual occasion in my childhood home. After a special breakfast of Eggs à la Goldenrod, my mother and father would stand at the front door—thrilled that summer was over for them too, I'm sure, but also because they respected and promoted the value of school for their children—and I would march off into the rich Indian Summer morning. I smell that promise again today; my skin crackles with a deep and familiar charge.

Maddy, her mom, and I park at the intersection of two broad streets and slip through a break in the cyclone fencing, where we make our way across the vast, grassy playing fields. Bagby's single-story buildings, two wings in an L shape, seem distant, a mirage. This is a typical 1950s public school, one of thousands built during California's Cold War prosperity. It is not in any way an imposing structure but seems, in fact, rather casual.

Today, young parents guide their toddler up and down a jungle gym in one of the play areas; a father and son take pitching practice at one of the backstops, the ball snapping the air when it smacks into a glove; under a drooping pine a teenage couple, deep in mid-snog, imagines themselves inviolable. And under the classroom's wide eaves, dozens of parents and students shuttle about, adding final touches to makeshift booths that are swathed in black and orange. By chance we've shown up on the day of Bagby's Fall Carnival, a necessary fundraising event. I'll learn that parents aren't allowed to call this a "Halloween" carnival, for obscurely nuanced and somewhat religious reasons, but will also learn, more dispiritingly, that this is only one of several fund-raisers Bagby parents will hold this year.

Maddy and Julie have raced ahead and taken over a second play yard. Maddy instantly sheds her thirteen-year-old cool and is suddenly much younger, sliding down slides, balancing along a low rail, dangling from monkey bars, swinging on swings, unable to resist. Julie, too, has regressed, it seems, into a more cautious parent; while she's clearly enjoying Maddy's exuberance, she stands close by, vigilant, ready to offer comfort or first aid.

Me, I'm stuck in the middle of the playing fields, attendant to the swath of the past that's revealed itself. Along with the simple and nostalgic memories Bagby holds for me—*I did this here, that there*—I find that many other and larger concerns gather around the school.

I attended school during California's golden age of education. Funded in large part by the prosperity of the state's military-industrial Cold War economy, our public schools were newly built, and fully staffed and funded, a great source of pride to the Union's most populous state. Between 1962 and 1975, when I was a public school student in grades K–12, California schools were invariably ranked number one in the nation by all measures. Today, the state's public schools are regularly ranked forty-eighth or forty-ninth.

I've long been dismayed by the prevailing conditions: overcrowded classrooms; drastic cuts to all but the most basic curricula; the deteriorating conditions of buildings and grounds; an emphasis on standardized test scores; the long exodus of excellent teachers, and the imminent threat to teachers' seniority and their unions; bloated and costly administrations; fractious public debates about educational content and pedagogical methods. The portrait is a most depressing one.

From this cloud of issues a single idea coalesces, one that has much been on my mind recently: the lack of the public's will to fund schools adequately. This trend began, in California at least, in 1978 with the passage of Proposition 13, which greatly reduced property taxes; public education took the brunt of the cuts. The voters' insistence on lower taxes, and our legislators' eagerness to comply, continued with the Reagan "tax revolt" of the 1980s and was not limited to California's schools. Today's fund-raiser at Bagby is too common a sight around the country; while touring schools as a kids' book author for the past several years, I've seen such fund-raisers not only across California but also in Vermont, Wisconsin, Washington, Oregon. Every time you see one car wash or bake sale, multiply that number by a thousand.

My concern for California's public schools, while at

root civic minded, arises from my own history there, a concern that is about more than test scores and global "workplace" competition. I was the first person from my working-class family to go to college, an opportunity made possible by the largesse and excellence of California's public schools, and that opportunity shaped my life in profound and enduring ways, offering me a future that was intellectually, imaginatively, democratically, and, yes, economically richer than I would have found otherwise.

More importantly, while I was benefiting from this public bounty, schools practically saved my life in a very personal way. I'm sure this claim sounds overdramatic, but it's hard for me to see it in any other terms. After the sudden death of my father when I was in junior high school, my life, both in school and out of it, took decidedly troubling turns, and there were several years when I was on the verge of "slipping through the cracks," of not "living up to my potential." I can only imagine how thin my life would have been, how limited my choices, if I had continued on that path. My schools—their teachers, administrators, and the very structures those schools offered—steered me to a course that made it possible for me to rescue myself. Yes, school saved my life.

I'm also a teacher, so my attention is always drawn to the classroom. Although I came to teaching late, and work mostly with adults, it is an art that has given me much joy and fulfillment, and I know I am a teacher only because of the long line of those who taught me. My teachers devoted immeasurable time and energy to their tasks—the creation of *daily* lesson plans; evenings and weekends swamped by checking students' homework; intense relationships with parents and students; continuing professional development—and they did so with only meager monetary or social benefits. Teachers, especially those in K–12, work as hard as they do to make a difference in the life of one student. Today, looking into the classrooms at Bagby and reliving my time there, I am appropriately moved by the realization that a teacher's work, too often ill regarded these days, begins and ends here, one teacher and one student entering a long conversation about the world.

I'm fortunate, I know, as a kids' book author, to be invited into schools, both public and private, rich and poor. I wish that every parent—maybe every adult— could spend a day at school now and then, an entire and regular day, to see the excitement that happens in the most basic classroom, the hunger of children to learn. We often speak of the "natural curiosity" of children, but to see it in action, twenty or thirty hands eagerly waving, can serve as an immediate reminder of what school actually does. Each of us has different memories of school, but no matter how we look back on those years—with joy or disdain—there was a time, during our K–12 years usually, when the classroom was an adventure for most of us, a form of luxury the world provided. From the middle of Bagby's playing fields, I can see hundreds of student-made decorations and projects and posters in classroom windows, clear signals of busy minds at work.

Of course, I'm a parent of a schoolchild, too. Maddy has just begun her high school applications, and many questions about her schooling occupy our time. She has been a fortunate student, attending, through the virtue of our modest income and attendant financial aid, two excellent "independent" (read: private) schools in San Francisco. As we go forward with her high school search, Maddy leading the charge, we have reentered a debate we've had since kindergarten: public or private? This year the decision may not be entirely ours, given our financial situation. As a family, we're excited about Maddy's high school; as a parent, I'm anxious. So much depends on . . .

I jog up to join Julie and Maddy at the carnival. We wander past the rickety booths. Cheesy games of chance—one twenty-five-cent ticket gets you three beanbags and a plastic spider ring if you sink the bags in a bucket. Homemade crafts: candles and corn wreaths and broomstick witches. The requisite sweets: coffee cakes and cookies and candied apples. Maddy's got her eye on a Bagby Barracudas T-shirt, a cartoon of a needle-nosed fish arching over the school's name. Why not? A small portion of these proceeds will benefit the school.

The money that's raised today, one mom tells me, will buy essential items for Bagby's classrooms—paper, pencils, books, art supplies. It's sad, she tells us, but it's what we have to do. I recall a bumper sticker that's been around for decades: *It will be a great day when our schools get all the money they need and the air force has to hold a bake sale to buy a bomber.*

Bagby's interior courtyards and classrooms are locked against vandals and other mischief, and the carnival huddles on a fringe of broken asphalt. It's quite feudal, this meager market on the edge of something that was once grand. It makes us all seem like paupers.

On our way to the car, near the far edge of the field, I turn back to the school and the crowd offering up their pocket change. In an instant all my larger concerns and grand ideas dissipate, and I'm swept away again, but more deeply this time, into my seven years at Bagby. I'm *assaulted* by the past; the world sparks and forges my memories.

I'm drawn into a vivid memory from second grade, one that's surfaced in my consciousness over the years and so is familiar. I don't so much *remember* that day and what it was like to be seven years old again; I *become* that child again.

I'm leaving school at the end of the day, standing on the sidewalk outside the low cyclone fence. It is a black and rain-driven day; I've never known a day so dark and rainy. I'm leaning into the wind in my yellow rain jacket, and there is the school, my school, its windows yellow lighted, teachers still in their classrooms.

That is all there is to the memory. The feeling that rises up out of the memory, however, is enormous, the bodily knowledge that it is here, at Bagby, that I was shaped, that the beginning of a long path that continues today started in this place, in this school, in that classroom there.

A Child's Garden

Soon after stopping by Bagby in the fall, a keen hunger to get closer to my school days rises, a desire to be inside those very same classrooms again, to see what has changed and what remains, to remind myself of what happens there. So I call Bagby's principal to arrange a visit while classes are in session. I am an alum, a writer, a teacher, I explain. Of course, she says.

It's been forty-nine years since I was last in this classroom, and I'm surprised to discover how large it is. Anticipating today's visit, I had expected my former kindergarten to appear diminutive, diminished in stature as one's childhood places so often are—the backyard a postage stamp now, the neighborhood streets oddly narrow. But the kindergarten feels vast, capacious, a town of its own, made bigger for all of its busyness. One group of children hammers and saws with plastic tools on a plastic workbench; four others, in plastic smocks, fingerpaint at easels; two are feeding the classroom pets, a fleet of guppies in a tank that is tantalizingly near

the tarantula terrarium; seven children are seated on the
floor in a circle around Miss Abbe, who is reciting words
that begin with the hard *c* sound: *cow, cat, cap;* in one
corner, hidden behind a low bookcase, a solitary child
daydreams her way into a picture book about jungle life.

Bagby Elementary has changed little over the decades,
architecturally at least, and what was Mrs. Moody's classroom in 1962 is the same size and shape it has always been,
the tiny chairs and tables just as tiny. I have changed, of
course. I'm nearly twice as tall now, and it may be that my
adult perspective allows me to appreciate the size of the
space, the blueprint of its possibilities.

A classroom announces its intentions in a visceral, architectural manner. If the room is dilapidated, unkempt,
undersupplied, it tells the student not to get comfortable here, that this is simply a place to endure, a place
to be frightened of. When a classroom is healthy, well
lighted, spacious, warm in the cold and cool in the
heat, and filled with objects that demand exploration,
it tells the student, this is *your* place; this is where you
are meant to thrive. Children always feel vulnerable to
the world, and in fact often are, either at home or in
their neighborhood, but the best classrooms dispel that
vulnerability, and can make children secure enough to
grow and change. The classroom's message is simple
but deeply resonant.

The ceilings of my old kindergarten, precisely as I
remember them, vault from low walls into an airy can-
opy, one that mimics the classroom's wild ambitions.
Along the eastern wall, large windows let in the morn-

ing light, and on the opposing wall, narrow windows temper the often harsh afternoon sun. The southern wall of the room is what I remember most, however, where ceiling-high windows rise up, cathedral-like, offering an unobstructed view of the sky. The room is a concrete metaphor for what education offers the student: *If you focus in this place, you will find larger worlds.*

The message is at once more cluttered and complex, too. The classroom walls are covered with maps and charts: California, the United States, the world, the solar system; colors and shapes and letters and animals. The walls are also covered with student artwork, so much so that the drawings overlap the windows: drawings of pigs, houses, flowers, a child's own view of the solar system. This tide of paper announces to students that they are gathered to focus on their work and the world equally, to see what they can make of it all.

This current classroom holds a bounty of tools and toys and supplies. Shelves of books, cubicles filled with games and puzzles and musical instruments, loads of crayons and paints and construction paper and easels and smocks, and yes, even a few computers. Along with the fish and Charlotte, the twenty-year-old tarantula, there are several terrariums of lush riparian plants. Such bounty says to the students—said to me when I was a child and to these students today—get to work, do things, make things.

The center of the classroom is an open area covered with colorful, rubbery, comfy pads made from recycled plastic and hooked together in a giant jigsaw puzzle. This is where the tribe gathers in community, in discussion, in reading, and in song. Around this town square, narrower and more purposeful spaces invite students to explore on their own.

Paired tables and loose chairs form working pods where small groups can huddle over a common task. Shelves and cubbies create narrow, maze-like alleys where students work under their own steam.

The teacher's desk, as it did in 1962, sits in a corner where low bookshelves create a semiprivate cubicle. Here intimate conferences can be held, and the teacher can sometimes be alone for a while.

In another corner there are two self-contained mini-rooms, a play kitchen and a carpenter's workshop, each made of plastic, each an enclosed space of solid, if limited, possibility. It doesn't matter, I suppose; children will fill up any space with whatever imagination they require. Still, I want these spaces to be less single minded, more than just kitchen or workshop. And then I see the blocks, the same ones I used to use. These blocks are cardboard flats that have been folded and tabbed into hollow bricks, each printed with a green or red pattern to make them look more like bricks (apparently some bricks are green). Most importantly, there are hundreds of them.

For me it was not only this new construction material that was so exciting when I was five, but also new builders to work with, troops of kids I'd never met before who were now in the classroom with me. This is one of the great movements of school life, an ever-expanding circle of fellow students and friends that continues to widen at each step along the way—elementary, junior

high, high school, college. So, armed with these blocks
and a cloud of new minds to put them to use, my fellow
kindergartners and I built things we might not have in-
vented on our own.

Some of our cardboard block constructions were
rather domestic. Laurie Riordan and I often built kitch-
ens, where we faithfully imitated the life we saw in our
homes, but later that year, because of our schooltime together, we would share a first kiss while walking home
together one day, a brand-new type of construction
for us. Bryan Jacques, Tommy Shaw, and I tended to
build workshops, where we would then create tools
to help us build other things. Some of our cardboard
block inventions were more fantastical, borrowed from
storybooks and TV—medieval castles, frontier forts,
underwater cities—and once Craig Chavez and I built a
time machine. What we most often built, however, in
Mrs. Moody's classroom, and what said the most about
who we were then and what school inspired in us, were
rocket ships. We were all *Sputnik* babies, born in 1957,
and our imaginations were a riot of astronauts and
planets; with a single basic shape, the block, we traveled
to the far reaches of the universe.

As ubiquitous as kindergarten is today, it is one of the
more recent evolutions in the history of schools, a concept first introduced in 1837 by the German educator
Friedrich Froebel.

The youngest of our children had long been educated outside the home, but only those few whose parents could afford it. Before the advent of kindergarten,

the manner in which the fortunate young were educated is one we might not recognize. In the West at least, the youngest students who were sent to school before Froebel's idea became established were treated as the young scholars they were meant to become, as if they were tiny adults. They were taught in "grammar" schools to read and write, to figure numbers, and to memorize and assemble the necessary facts.

In imperial Rome, for a brief time, there did exist the *ludus,* a course of study meant to prepare even younger students for the grammar school. The simple translation of *ludus* is "play," but the pedagogy of the *ludus* was quite similar to that of Rome's grammar schools. At the age of seven, students were instructed in the names of letters before they saw them written out, and only then would they learn to write them. From letters they moved on to syllables, then whole words, and finally sentences. There was also instruction in simple arithmetic. And as in many educational institutions before the middle of the twentieth century, classroom discipline in the *ludus* could be physical, harsh, and often random.

Froebel's kindergarten was a radical departure. The idea for it, he claimed later, came to him while he was out walking one day; he looked up and said, "Eureka! A garden where children can grow!" Literally, of course, *kindergarten* is German for "children's garden." What Froebel wished to introduce to the classroom was a spirit of friendliness toward the child.

Like most Eureka moments, however, Froebel's was

not entirely spontaneous. He had been a student of Johann Heinrich Pestalozzi, a self-taught Swiss educator who believed that children were not merely short adults but creatures who required training appropriate to their emotional and cognitive development. Pestalozzi had been, in his turn, influenced by Jean-Jacques Rousseau, particularly his novel *Émile, ou de l'éducation,* whose main character is lovingly prepared for society rather than tossed into its teeming streets. Of course, Froebel, Pestalozzi, and Rousseau were not only shapers of their times but obedient to them as well. Their educational theories are impossible without the growth of Enlightenment thinking in Europe, which would give birth to the ideals of the American and French revolutions, the Romantic movement, and the burgeoning liberalism that accompanied the onset of the Industrial Revolution. The individual, even a child, was now seen as having an innate value.

Froebel opened his first Universal German Kindergarten in 1840. If the pedagogy was to be different here, then the shape of the classroom had to make room for that difference. So Froebel abolished the classic arrangement of desks in rows and created an open design any of today's kindergartners would recognize. He also insisted that the classroom not be contained by four walls. Children exploring nature on their own, hands-on, was a central Froebelian notion; field trips and recess were an integral component of one's education.

As revolutionary as these spatial changes were the objects Froebel brought into his classroom: spheres, cubes, cylinders, rings, triangles. With these basic shapes, children could create larger and more complex patterns, as I would later travel to Alpha Centauri in a rocket made of cardboard blocks. Froebel's children were only playing, it seemed, but in a deep manner; they were using their natural impulses to create and combine, rather than being directed by a teacher's "lessons." Play, it turned out, was educational.

Froebel's favorite object was the sphere, but let's call it what it is, a ball. Froebel saw the ball as a shape that represented the unity of all creation, but in his practical teaching, he did not make it abstract. It was simply a ball, and it belonged to the child. Yet a ball also taught about the concepts of over and under, near and far, up and down. We learn, Froebel posited, with our minds and our bodies in unison.

The idea and practice of kindergarten caught on quickly, especially in the United States, where in the decades after the Civil War, it increasingly became the norm in both rural and urban areas. In the early 1900s, under the influence of philosopher and educational reformer John Dewey, the learning of letters and numbers was added to the kindergarten curriculum, though the ball, and all that play, remained central. When I walk past my daughter's K–8 school today, red rubber balls from the kindergarten playground often find their way over the fence and under the wheels of parked cars. The kindergartners call out, "Hey, mister, can you get our ball, please, please, please?" I heave it back over the high fence, happy to help them learn. Over and under, high and low, far and near.

One central and Froebel-inspired lesson offered to me in kindergarten has proved to be an essential and long-lasting one, at least to me: a good nap is important.

When my mother escorted me into Mrs. Moody's kindergarten that September, I brought along, as instructed, only one thing, my napping mat. This was a carpet remnant my father had picked up, slate blue and barely big enough for me to fit on.

I was enrolled in the morning session, a rather short day; I arrived at nine and returned home at noon. In the first hour we engaged in a number of indoor activities, after which, wrung out from all that fingerpainting or pickup sticks, we would have a snack, which was always the same: graham crackers washed down with slightly warm milk from miniature waxed cartons. Lulled sleep-ward by the warm milk, we unrolled our mats on the speckled brown linoleum and slept side by side, twenty or so little bean bodies breathing together. I often found it difficult to get to sleep; here I was, as in some happy cult, napping with a herd of strangers. Mrs. Moody spent nap time at her desk, reading novels and occasionally shushing us.

Refreshed from our naps—twenty minutes?—we were turned loose in a dedicated playground that was fenced off from the older grades; there we ran and played until released at noon.

What was not to like about kindergarten? Every day I got to play with a cadre of new friends in a room over-stuffed with objects I could only think of as "toys." Art at the drop of a hat; music every day; rockets to be constructed; endless shelves of books. A snack and a nap, then time on some very nice, if not, in retrospect, dangerous monkey bars and swings that hovered over beds of soft tanbark. The short day of kindergarten seemed just enough novelty, a few hours away from the unstructured space and time of home. I was happy to be home again, but excited to return to school the next day.

Kindergarten seemed to me a place of great riches, and I still believe, after the many other classrooms I've sat in, that the classroom, no matter the grade level, remains luxurious. Our English word *school* comes from the Greek *scholē*, a school or a discussion held there, but the same root carries an earlier meaning, "leisure, or spare time." From "leisure," the word evolved to denote a discussion conducted at leisure, which in turn became the place where such discussions were held. Whether it's a kindergartner singing a song, a high school student studying physics before going to college, or an adult taking a botany course for personal edification, once in a classroom, all students enjoy the privilege of education, set off for those hours from the noise and intents of life, luxuriant in learning, separate from but focused on the wider world.

The etymology fits socially, too. For centuries school was the privilege of the privileged. Today, when elementary education is nearly universal, we might forget, but

shouldn't, that schooling was until quite recently impossible for the vast majority of children. In nineteenth-
century England, at the time one of the most prosperous
and literate nations on earth, only one in three children
attended school. In the United States, school was not
compulsory in all states until 1920.

Today, UNESCO estimates that at least 72 million
children worldwide are prevented from attaining the
most basic education. Of the many factors that keep
these children out of school—political, religious, gender,
and ethnic discriminations—the leading one, by far, is
poverty. It is a startling and troubling number—72 million children excluded from school—if only because so
many hundreds of millions of children do go to school.
The thought of a child *not* in school seems undeniably
wrong; school has become an expected luxury, a fundamental human right.

While I loved the idea of starting school, the prospect
was not without anxiety. My older sister and brother,
both in high school by the time I began kindergarten,
went off to school each day, and of course I always
wanted to do what they did. But they spoke of sports
and dates and dances, and complained about something
called homework. Before kindergarten began, I really
had no idea what school was all about, only that I was
expected to go, the next step in growing up. Like most
of what my teenage brother and sister did, school was
desired but mysterious.

When it came time for Maddy to attend preschool—

there was no preschool in the world I grew up in—my wife and I had at our disposal a number of picture books about the first days and weeks of school. In these books there is always the anxiety of the unknown on the part of the child—the child represented as panda, monkey, fish—but over the course of the story, that anxiety is mitigated by the excitement of the actual. None of these stories ends in disaster, though I suspect this is not true of all first days.

To divert my school anxiety, and in an attempt to foster my excitement, my mother suggested we visit Bagby's principal the week before classes started. What was a principal? I asked. The king of the school, my mother said, an apt comparison but one that proved frightening. I still occasionally suffer the dream I had before going to meet the principal. In an enormous hall, on a throne on a dais, the principal waits for us to approach, a scene straight out of *The Wizard of Oz*. In the dream, my mother and I never make it to the throne, we are always approaching. Today my mother insists we did meet with the principal, but I recall nothing of that conference, only the approach.

I'm still susceptible to other school-anxiety dreams, too. I'm not ready for the test, or naked, or naked and not ready for the test, or standing naked on a table and still not ready for the test. I have similar dreams from a teacher's point of view, usually at the beginning of a new semester. I cannot find the class roster in a shower of millions of pieces of paper, hours go by, students walk out in disgust. School remains for me, and I suspect for many others, that place where we will be judged and found lacking, a garden from which we may be expelled. School is often where we first become public, where forces beyond our knowing shape our destinies. Or more simply, school is the first time we leave home.

When Maddy began preschool at Belvedere Montessori, she was already a pretty game child, and couldn't wait, it seemed, to spend her days behind the school's little purple door. We had visited the inviting classroom, a converted garage/basement in San Francisco's Haight-Ashbury, and Maddy was chomping at the bit to get started. Her first day turned out more difficult for her mother and me than for her. "Good-bye," she said, running off to join her new pals without a single glance back; her mother and I managed to hold our tears until we were in the car.

Maddy's happy departures continued for about six weeks, until one morning she suddenly turned to me, abandonment in her eyes, and begged to go back home; she latched on to me and sobbed and sobbed. This keening went on every morning for a week, until it passed as mysteriously as it came. The preschool's head, Barbara Alexander, explained, as she tore Maddy from my arms and pushed me out the door, that such belated anxieties were common, almost always around six weeks. It seems that the child, at first delighted by the novelty of school, eventually realizes that she will be going there *every* day. School is not a diversion or an accessory, but a new way of life.

It's frightening to go to school for the first time, or

to a new school, or junior high or high school or college. Each step on this journey requires a big leap in one's life. School intends to take you away from your home, place you in the public sphere, introduce you to wider vistas. Such leaps are thrilling, but terror lives in them, too. The yet unknown is the destination of school's journey.

I must admit that I remember my kindergarten teacher, Mrs. Moody, in only the most general outline. I know that I thought of her as "old" back then, but a five-year-old's "old" is not reliable; Mrs. Moody might have been thirty or sixty. Cat's-eye glasses and a beehive hairdo; long woolen skirt, silk blouse; her soft but powerful presence. Mrs. Moody was simply the adult who was in charge of me, and I gave little thought to her beyond that. Which is not to say she was not a crucial person in my life: she was my teacher. Every minute of those short kindergarten days, she kept me hard at work with organized play, games and exercises that led me from one concept to another, building new structures in my brain and body, new ways of knowing the world. It's not so important that she taught me this thing or that thing, but that she taught me, as the best teachers do, how to teach myself.

In my memory, fittingly, it is Mrs. Moody's classroom, the child's garden she tended, that prevails. Mrs. Moody kneels primly, while we sit around her "Indian style," as we called it. She claps a steady beat, chanting ritually, as we chant with her, "two, four, six, eight . . ." by twos through twenty, then again from the beginning. Did I know my numbers before I started kindergarten? Well, I am learning them now. Or I'm supposed to be learning them.

But I am not paying attention. I'm staring at the wall above Mrs. Moody's beehive, where the letters of the alphabet march along with great vigor, led by *A* for Alligator and his drum major's baton. I have veered off course again, which will be a common complaint of my teachers for many years.

It's not my fault, really, that my attention has strayed; let me blame the classroom's bounty. I'm staring at the letters of the alphabet because we've been learning them all year, and I'm intrigued. *A* is for Alligator; *B* is for Bear; *C* is for Cat. Whether Mrs. Moody knows it or not, I'm learning in my distraction.

Today, Miss Abbe's students sit in the age-old circle, all facing her. The few changes in this room over the years are minor. There are the comfy mats—those would have been nice back then—and Miss Abbe wears jeans, which would have been unthinkable in 1962, but she still sits on the floor with her charges. What matters has remained.

Each of Miss Abbe's students holds a stiff piece of cardboard that is shaped like a boot and punctuated with holes, through which they all thread a long red lace. "Now we go over; now we go through. Now we go under; now we go through." Repeat.

One girl, however, has stopped threading and chanting, and having risen to her knees, is staring far away. I recognize her gaze. She is fixed on the parade of alphabet letters above Miss Abbe's head; these letters do not march in a band, as mine did, but they are dancing, albeit in backward baseball caps—Aardvark, Beaver, Cheetah. This girl may be getting ready for the next big leap. She may have just now realized that *A* is, indeed, for Aardvark, that *A* is, in fact, the first letter in the *word* Aardvark. She may be on the verge of reading.

Ride Fast, Betty.
Ride Fast, Tom.

It's a brief walk from Bagby's kindergarten to its first-grade classrooms—past the school's offices: secretary, nurse, principal—but when I was five, this hallway seemed an epic journey. Kindergarten had been a world apart. Each morning we entered the kindergarten class-room through a door on the far side of the school and played in our own pint-sized playground. But at times that year I could hear and feel the percussive crush of the big kids at their recess, or catch a glimpse of the fourth graders at work, seated in rows and attentive to the teacher at the blackboard, maybe reading at their desks. Kindergartners have longings, too, and I longed to be with the big kids, in the future.

On the first day of first grade I marched to school confidently in new shoes, shirt, pants, and of course, new underwear—nothing quite recalls school for me like the smell of cotton underwear fresh from the package. I walked to school alone that day—my choice; I was a big kid now. There I was greeted by Mrs. Talley, who, in her cat's-eye glasses and beehive hairdo, soothingly resembled Mrs. Moody.

Everything else about first grade was different, though. The day ended at three, so I took a lunch box with me, round topped and red, painted to look like a barn. Instead of entering the classroom right off, we congregated on the asphalt play area near our classroom door, girls in one line, boys in the other; hundreds of us, first through sixth graders, noised and tussled until a whistle was blown, the lines resolved themselves into silence, and we marched into a new year.

The most obvious change that September was the classroom itself. The cheerful open floor plan had been replaced by neat rows of individual desks, assigned to us alphabetically. Mrs. Talley's own desk, enormous and metallic, sat at the front of the room, and on the wall behind this was a new contrivance, the blackboard.

My first-grade classroom did contain art supplies, of course—construction paper, crayons, scissors, pots of amber glue and white paste, buckets of cloth scraps and colored feathers and pipe cleaners—but they were off to one side, hidden away, and aimed, it seemed clear, at more constrained, desk-friendly projects. I carry a sharp sadness that after kindergarten we never indulged in "fingerpainting" again, that messy and odorous delight.

What prevailed in the bounty of the first-grade classroom were more scholarly supplies, however. Rolled maps and charts above the blackboard; globes of the earth and moon, a miniature solar system; shelves of individual books, along with stacks of multiple copies of books; boxes of thick pencils and pads of pulpy, blue-lined writing paper; rafts of 3-D math puzzles, flash cards, cardboard clocks for learning to tell time. It was clear on entering first grade that, while art might be a worthy digression, we were to focus more purposefully now: reading, writing, arithmetic.

The number functions we studied in the lower years of elementary school were technically arithmetic, but we only ever called this subject math. Math would never be my strongest subject, especially later when I progressed to algebra (the same is true for my wife; Maddy, alas, has inherited the same "challenge," as we call it). But math was not without its allure. As with all subjects when they were first introduced, math captured my broadening imagination, especially its somewhat magical properties: the joy of addition, the ache of subtraction, the mystery of multiplication, and the undeniable terror of division.

In kindergarten we had learned to count, an endless chant of numbers, a long string of mathematical syntax riveted deep into the body, but in first grade, we would begin to put these numbers in motion, writing increasingly complex sentences with them.

Froebel's early concept that concrete learning abets abstract formulation gradually found its way out of the kindergarten classroom and into the higher grades, and in Mrs. Talley's class we learned to add and subtract with a host of three-dimensional aids, which I could only think of as games. My favorite of these was Mr. Math, a red plastic stick figure three feet high, wearing a jaunty white boater, whose fingers and toes were long plastic digits that could be moved and removed. If you wanted to solve the equation $4 + 3 =$ ___, you put four white fingers on one hand, then added three to the other. Counting on Mr. Math's fingers became counting on my own, and each time I performed a task, the calculation burrowed deeper into my brain.

All that year we added and added, single-digit equations, the same ones over and over—there are only so many combinations. Then we subtracted, taking away smaller single digits from larger ones. In second grade we added and subtracted numbers in the tens and hundreds, and learned to "carry," though the equations were basically the same. Once you've learned the trick, there's little to do but practice.

Over the next six years we continued the study of math through simple, repetitive exercises. In third grade there was a season when I wrote, over and over, the numbers from 1 to 1,000 on gridded sheets of paper, one hundred grids to each sheet. There was some contest to this; whoever wrote up to 1,000 the most times won something, perhaps a prize as ephemeral as the winner's name written in chalk on the blackboard.

From second through fifth grades, I spent hours and hours memorizing my "times tables": $2 \times 2 = 4$, $2 \times 3 = 6$ . . . all the way to a satisfying $12 \times 12 = 144$. In class, we chanted these numbers together, along with hours of recitation at home, and sometimes, without thinking, while walking around the neighborhood, my brain simply clicked on and I chanted alone, unable to stop. There are many critics of rote learning—the charge: it stifles creativity—and admittedly, I found these exercises painfully boring, but rote learning does have its uses. Memorizing the times tables is not about intelligence, or critical or creative thinking; it is about inculcation, branding the brain. Today, when I'm required to multiply, I look up and away—a natural instinct—gazing somewhere into my past, and there are the numbers, waiting for me, the chant still running through my head and my body. When I was first learning multiplication, I had trouble memorizing 8×7, and even now, multiplying those two numbers, I must pause an extra moment for the answer to appear, stuck in the same place I got stuck in elementary school. But the calculation and result are both there, if a little slow.

A common discussion in my math classrooms up through high school centered on the utility of math. We frequently demanded of our teachers, when would we ever use any of this arcane language in the "real" world? Mostly they answered with appeals to our sense of security, that every "career," every business enterprise, would require this knowledge. I was perhaps the most vocal of these accusers, and scoffed at my teachers' pragmatic defenses—didn't we have adding machines, slide rules, those new pocket calculators, maybe even someday our own computers? The truth is, my teachers were right. Years of repetitive chanting, worksheets, and quizzes on arithmetic and fractions and, yes, even algebra, did prepare me for the mathematical demands of the real world, from household budgets to business charts and graphs, to measuring for new window treatments. I still do much of my "figuring" in my head, thanks to all that repetition.

While math intrigued me in first grade, it was nothing compared to the thrill of discovering the other fundamental skill Mrs. Talley would teach me: reading. When I walked in that first morning, there, on each of our desks, was something brand new, a textbook. I knew about books, of course, at home and from the public library, and kindergarten had been flush with them, picture books by the hundreds, books that were read to us and that we thumbed through independently. Like most kids that age, I had begun to read on my own a little—street signs, baseball and football trading cards, a favorite storybook—picking out words and phrases here and there, if only through repetition and context.

I don't remember the first word I read on my own, but I'm certain of my daughter's: *zoo*. We were not going to the zoo that day, but were driving past Golden Gate Park's panhandle, where advertising banners fluttered from lampposts. "Zoo," Maddy intoned rather seriously, then squealed with delight at her achievement. Julie and I turned to her with astonishment, and Maddy squealed some more. "Zoo," we all said, and then we talked about the zoo and the last time we had been there. The world, the memory of the world, and the signs for that memory, all converged at that moment.

Life is full of mysterious signs, and children wish, as we all do, to decode their mysteries.

But at my desk in Mrs. Talley's room, *My Little Red Story Book* announced itself as an entirely new machine. Despite the title's first-person possessive pronoun, each student's copy remained the property of the school. But it was *mine* for now. This book was eight inches tall and six inches wide, so vertical, rather than horizontal like the picture books I was then used to, and it was smaller, too, more fitted to the hands than the lap. While *My Little Red Story Book* did contain color illustrations, it was clear from the way the text captured the page that this was a book meant for *reading.*

It is with reading, we have long been convinced as a culture, that education begins, in every subject, whether science, music, history, or art. Even the study of math, at least in its earliest years, requires the ability to read: John has 5 cookies and Mary has 7, but their 2 friends, Polly and Peter, stop by for snack time; if each child is to get an equal amount of cookies . . .

Bagby is an "elementary" school, by which we mean the basic elements—reading and writing. In the United States, elementary schools are sometimes still called "grammar" schools. We begin with reading.

Despite the initial excitement over *My Little Red Story Book,* I did not become a true reader until I was in high school and ready for the reading lust that would then overwhelm me. It was not just learning how to read that prepared me for my late-onset reading addiction, but the schools themselves that had prepared

me. From kindergarten on up, we were always surrounded by books, both in and out of the classroom,
in school libraries, of course, and through Scholastic
Book Club books we purchased in the classroom
and took home. There wasn't a corner of school that
wasn't filled with books.

When I visit the Marguerite Archer Collection of
Historic Children's Materials at San Francisco State
University, it is a storm-tossed Wednesday, and the
near-black sky draws everything in the world closer, a
perfect day to journey into my past and to immerse
myself in the great tide of material the teaching of reading has produced. The Archer collection contains over
thirty-five hundred items, some dating back to 1776: alphabet books, linen and board books, shaped books (as
in shaped like a dog or a fire truck), etiquette guides for
the young, sheet music, poetry, early readers, picture
books, children's periodicals, games and toys, movable
books (read "pop-up" books), ephemera (flashcards and
handouts, etc.), and of course, reading primers.

In a cramped cubicle, I open two boxes of California
public school textbooks from the 1960s. I've been given
the entire afternoon to look through them, a permission that feels very much like "free reading" did when
I was in school, a timeless space in which to disappear.

When I open the boxes I am transported by the scent
of paper, this particular blend of paper. Even under the
dust, and perhaps a bit of mold, I smell my school days.
As I unpack the boxes, I find my other senses leading

me into the past—the sharp crinkle of ruffled pages, the tooth of the blue-white paper, the familiar heft of these books in my hand, the rich crimson, apple-lime, and royal blue of the covers. I lean in and take a deeper whiff, inhale my childhood, animate the past that is long gone but always with me.

This is as close to time travel as I'm likely to get; the memory is inescapable. Several of us are seated in a half circle around Mrs. Talley, and we have our books on our laps. She holds her teacher's edition open, shows us the page where we are to begin. She reads; we read in response: "Ride fast, Betty. Ride fast, Tom." We read slowly, purposefully, as if the words were fragile.

In the library cubicle, I unpack the boxes and arrange the books by grade. This is where my reading life began, and to see these books, to be flooded by these memories, is a personal archaeology, an excavation of the cave where my brain was rewired and my mind constructed.

My Little Red Story Book, published by Ginn and Company, is a forty-six-page paperback bound with black cloth tape; the edition I used in 1963 was first published in 1957. Written by Odille Ousley and David H. Russell, with illustrations by Ruth Steed, each of the book's eleven stories concerns a suburban family who live in a little white house on Cherry Street. There's Tom and Betty, who are a little older than the book's readers (kids like to "read up"); Susan, the younger sister; Mother and Father, ever busy; Flip, the family dog; and Bunny, Susan's stuffed rabbit.

There's also a real pony named Pony, though there's

never any explanation of where it stays, nor how it's fed, nor who cleans up after it. Pony is simply trotted out when the family needs something fun to do.

The cover of *My Little Red Story Book* says much about how a reading primer both reflects and shapes its readers. Steed's four-color cover illustration—Tom and Betty and Susan watch Bunny ride a toy airplane that is suspended from an apple tree's bough—is right out of Norman Rockwell, but the image is set against a design that points to a bright future. The book's title appears in a sans serif, ultramodern typeface on a crayon-red background, while the left half of the cover is interrupted by a custard-yellow, atomic-age parabola that seems to sweep the characters into orbit.

Each story opens with a large illustration of the main character or event, below which is the title: "Tom," "Betty," "Susan," "Flip," "Mother," "The Airplane," "Pony," "The Apple," "Susan and the Toys," "Tom and the Toys," "The Toys."

When the story begins, two to four lines of text appear below a smaller illustration carefully composed to make sense of the words and their context. The characters and their actions appear on a white background, with only a few hints of landscape—the eave of a roof, a snag of bushes, a stairway railing. The reader remains focused on the immediate context, and the stories use the repetition and variation of words and sentences to evince that context. According to the Teacher's Edition, new words are added as the story progresses, but no more than one per page. By the end of *My Little Red Story*

Book, nineteen new words have entered the reader's vocabulary.

Here is the complete text of "The Airplane," a tale I remember with surprising clarity:

> Mother! Mother!
> Come and see Tom.
>
> See the airplane, Mother.
> See Tom and the airplane.
>
> See Bunny, Mother.
> Bunny can ride.
> See Bunny ride.
> Bunny can ride the airplane.
>
> See the airplane, Susan.
> Bunny can ride the airplane.
> Bunny can ride fast.
>
> Ride fast, Bunny.
> Ride, Bunny, ride.

Repetition, variation, and visual context are still the methods by which beginners learn to read. We start small, and always have—it is how we get to greater things.

There was nothing more grand, when I was six, than *My Little Red Story Book.* My parents, both my mother and father, read to me at night—my favorite was a book

I still have, *The Tall Book of Fairy Tales,* from which I also read to Maddy—a habit that promoted comfort as much as anything else. But to be able to read, all by myself, the words "Ride fast, Bunny," that seemed nothing less than magic.

William McGuffey published *The Eclectic First Reader for Young Children with Pictures* in 1836, and his later primers, through grade six, along with spelling books and works on grammar and rhetoric, were a staple in American schools until at least 1920. McGuffey readers have sold over 120 million copies, a staggering number that puts these textbooks right up there with the Bible on the all-time best-seller list. Even today, the primers sell around thirty thousand copies a year, in facsimile and revised editions, and are still used to teach reading to some private and homeschool students.

McGuffey primers start with the most basic element, the alphabet, which is produced on a single page in uppercase letters, then on a second page in lowercase. After this introduction, the methods are the same as *My Little Red Storybook:* repetition and variation, with contextual illustrations on each page.

> A cat A rat
> A cat and a rat.
> A rat and a cat.
> The cat has a rat.

The Eclectic First Reader also contains pronunciation guides for each set of new words and sounds, along with examples of the text in cursive handwriting. Elocution and penmanship were deemed necessary skills in McGuffey's America.

The original McGuffey primers emphasized the author's strict Calvinism. At the end of the original *First Reader* was this somewhat unsettling stanza:

> All you do and all you say,
>   He can see and hear;
> When you work and when you play,
>   Think the Lord is near.

The publishers of the McGuffey readers subtracted most of the religious matter just after the Civil War, when waves of immigrants added new religious and cultural textures to the country's "melting pot." This was a sound business decision because it made the books more desirable to a wider range of school districts. But the removal of overt dogma also reinforced a central tenet of the nineteenth century's increasingly progressive educational theories: let readers learn to read for themselves, first of all, so that they might choose their own beliefs.

Last year, when touring my daughter's new middle school, San Francisco Friends School, I was delighted to find stacks of new books in the classrooms. Not just individual books culled from the school's library, nor subject-centered textbooks, but classroom sets of novels, memoirs, plays. There, in the coat closet, were twenty fresh copies—fittingly—of Ray Bradbury's *Fahrenheit 451*, as well as stacks of Mildred Taylor's *Roll of Thunder, Hear My Cry,* Jon Krakauer's *Into the Wild,* and Shakespeare's *The Tempest.* I knew immediately that I was going to like the school.

Today we assume, rather blithely, a bounty of books in the classroom. Yet even with the widespread success of McGuffey in the nineteenth century, it was primarily urban schools, those supported by broad-based taxes, that benefited from consistent, focused, and plentiful reading material.

In the second half of that century, when the United States had a larger percentage of enrolled students than any other nation, and when new schools were appearing at an unprecedented rate, books in the classroom were still relatively scarce. At that time, 75 percent of American students attended one-room schoolhouses, these established and constructed by the rural communities they served, and independent of state or federal oversight and funding. The schools were constructed, teachers hired, and families asked to contribute whatever books they might spare. Students in the same one-room school might be reading from widely different texts—the Bible, a farmer's almanac, a volume of Shakespeare, the Sears Roebuck catalog, maybe a Dickens novel.

In the main, though, it was the teacher who owned the school's few books. Along with community donations, she might have one primer to share with the class, or a dictionary, maybe an atlas, a small bundle of novels. In 1846, when Olive Isbell opened a school at Mission

Santa Clara in California, she had no books whatsoever. So she improvised: she wrote the alphabet on the backs of her students' hands. The ink she used was permanent, and given the bathing habits of the time, the alphabets might last weeks or months.

Isbell's predicament was neither new nor rare. Before the Gutenberg revolution, when all books were copied by hand, students rarely touched any books; books were simply too expensive and there were too few of them. In order to learn to read, students were read to, the teacher "lecturing," from the Latin root, "to read." Paintings, drawings, and engravings of the classroom from Rome through the nineteenth century illustrate this.

Early students might have the opportunity to practice writing with a stylus on a wax tablet, or with a piece of gypsum on a slate, but even paper and ink were too costly for the everyday doodling we now take for granted. Before Gutenberg, a student might be allowed to read on his own by copying, by hand of course, one of his teacher's few books. This educational moment for the student was, in many cases, also a chance for the teacher to earn a little spare cash; student-copied books were then sold into a demand-heavy market.

Being read to, as comforting as it can be, is not the most efficient method for the teaching of reading. In the English-speaking world, beginning in the fifteenth century, there was, for nearly four hundred years, a simple and inexpensive teaching aid that helped those few students lucky enough to attend grammar school.

The hornbook was a paddle-shaped object on which

were written the basics of a grammar school education. At the top of the hornbook was the entire alphabet, followed by a table of vowels in combination with
consonants—*ab, ac, ad,* and so on. Below this was the
Trinitarian formula—"in the name of the Father and of
the Sonne and the Holy Ghost, Amen"—below which
was the Lord's Prayer, below which were Roman nu-
merals. These texts were printed on a sheet of parch-
ment, which was mounted on a paddle usually made of
wood, though sometimes of leather or ivory. To protect
the text, a transparent leaf of boiled and flattened horn—
cattle or goat or sheep—was affixed. A leather strap attached the hornbook to the student's wrist or waist.

What's surprising is how little the hornbook changed
over four hundred years. Nearly every extant hornbook, or description of one, carries exactly the same
text. Shakespeare, perhaps the most successful grammar
school graduate of all time, mentions one in *Love's Labor's
Lost,* twisting its simple text into an ironic and somewhat
sexual barb, of course.

Swaddled in memory, I spend the afternoon in the
Archer collection, rereading my old Ginn and Co. textbooks. I'm stunned to think how many children learned
to read out of Ginn primers, here in California and other
states, as well as Canada. Stunned, also, to discover that
each individual volume was held over the years by so
many hands. One copy of *My Little Green Story Book,* according the checkout stamp in the back, was used by at
least fifteen students in three different classrooms.

Seated in the library, the rain still pelting, I work my

way through my elementary education. Toward the end of first grade, when we were done with the paperback *Red, Green,* and *Blue* storybooks, we switched to hardcovers, with *Under the Apple Tree* and *Open the Gate,* and beyond that to *Around the Corner, Come with Us, Finding New Neighbors, Roads to Everywhere, Trails to Treasure,* and *Wings to Adventure*—from Cherry Street to spiral galaxies. The titles speak not only of the promise of these books but also of the promise of school itself.

It's clear to me that Ginn readers were not *my* childhood, but they spoke to me, back then, of childhood as a world of its own, because, through this adventure in reading, I began to form an understanding of who I was, where I actually lived, and where I might go.

Out of Ginn's idealized world, I began to delineate the real world. Ginn's authors and editors were clearly East Coast people. On Cherry Street, summers are green and lush, fall is orange and leafy, winter is a snowman, spring a bed of bright flowers. This East Coast parade of seasons couldn't be more different from California's turning wheel, where summer is arid and brown, there are few leaves to rake in the fall, it rains throughout winter and spring, and never snows. And until later in the 1960s, all of Ginn's characters were white, of course, though I went to school with children of many different shades. But reading the ideal, and pressing it against the actual, is a form of reading, too—reading not merely a book but the world.

The Archer collection will be closing soon, and when I begin to pack up these pieces of my past, my body drags me into yet another memory. I pick up a stack of books, and they fall immediately to my side, my arm fitting naturally around them; this was how I used to carry my school books every day. In an age before backpacks, there were two possible methods for carrying one's books: the guy carry, like an ape, arm hanging down; and the girl carry, books held safely against the chest. As a child I often used the girl carry, but only when no one else was around; it was the wiser and more comfortable of the two methods.

The weight of these books tugs me deeper into memory. I am walking home from Mrs. Talley's first grade, a binder and two books held close, and there, in a perfect childhood sky, is an airplane, one of the navy's Cold War sub chasers that passed over my neighborhood every two minutes. I look up. I whisper the word "airplane," and the word appears typed in my brain. The word and the world become one.

Blackboard

My first teacher crush came in second grade with Miss Cleveland. She was clearly younger than Mrs. Moody and Mrs. Talley, and I thought she was "really pretty." My adoration was so complete that I sometimes suffered on her behalf. Each morning Miss Cleveland read aloud to us, and once, while she read from *The Wind in the Willows,* I was determined not to interrupt her, so I put off asking permission to use the restroom until it was too late. I must not have been alone in my adoration, for when I wet myself that day, providing a prime opportunity for the cruelty of my fellow students to rise up, my classmates noted my accident but remained reverently silent.

Near the end of my second-grade year, Miss Cleveland left us to get married, a betrayal so shocking I cannot recall who replaced her those last few months. I made Miss Cleveland a going-away card, we had a party with cake and decorations, and tears were shed.

But today, when I peer in the small window of that

second-grade classroom, I find, despite my boyhood
ardor and its powerful remnants, that I am unable to picture Miss Cleveland except as a silhouette: she stands at
the blackboard with her back to us, her exquisite, loop-
ing cursive flourishing there, an example to us all. We
had learned to print our letters in first grade, on pulp-
filled Big Chief pads, writing with pencils the size of a
cat's leg, but now we were using ink!

Miss Cleveland was undoubtedly young and pretty,
but that's not the only reason my affection for her remains. In kindergarten we were shepherded by our
teacher, and in first grade, we spent most of our time in
groups, heads bent over books, or adding and subtract-
ing with Mr. Math. But in second grade, we spent most
of our time looking at Miss Cleveland, the blackboard
behind her, and it is this image, the teacher in front of
the blackboard, that dominates memories of my classrooms up through and into college. The blackboard is not
merely a convenient teaching tool; it becomes a focus for
the student's mind, and a reflection of that mind, both individually and for the larger class. The blackboard is not
an object that is merely stared at; the student sees beyond
what's written there, to the larger world.

In order to mark the blackboard with the appropriate
lines and spaces for our "handwriting" lessons, Miss
Cleveland used a wood-and-wire contraption that held
three pieces of chalk, drawing it silently across the
board (though this memory may be revisionist; how
can one write on a blackboard silently?). The three parallel lines she made kept the letters from straying too

high or low, and kept the intermediate loops uniform
and contained. As Miss Cleveland formed each letter on
the board, describing aloud the slope and intent of each
stroke, we imitated her at our desks, writing on individual leaves of paper.

We began with the alphabet, upper- and lowercases
of each letter at first, then we learned to string letters together with formulaic connective strokes, magically re-
vealing words that were more like small paintings than
the crowded bus stops of printed letters. I very much did
not like this course of study. It was tedious and repetitive, and as a left-handed writer, I found it messy and
frustrating. But as with both math and reading, subjects
also first gained through tedious repetition, proficiency
soon arrived, and I could, if not neatly, write lines and
lines of flowing sentences. This is the advantage of cursive, that one need not interrupt the flow of thought at
each letter.

My daughter's introduction to handwriting was quite
different. At her Montessori-style preschool, she was
taught to print when she was four, and was soon keeping a journal, albeit one based on the loosest of phonet-
ics, all before she learned to read a single word from a
book. In first grade, at French American International
School, Maddy learned cursive under the classical French
method, a draconian approach that verges on punishment at times. This method relies heavily on *dictées,*
where the students write out what the teacher reads to
them; *dictées* continue for years in French schools, not
only for the improvement of one's cursive but for spelling, grammar, and other aspects of writing. Maddy, too,

hated learning to write, but her handwriting today, and her control of a pen or stylus in any medium, is considerable; she has a repertoire of writing and drawing styles that makes me envious.

In today's frequently rancorous public debates over what constitutes "necessary" or "marketable" skills for our youngest students, cursive writing is often deemed superfluous and in some school districts has been supplanted by "keyboarding." Keyboarding does seem a necessary skill, but what might be lost when handwriting disappears? Handwriting is essential, and in its own way infinite. When the power goes out, pens and paper work just fine.

My mother recently recovered from her garage two "novels" I wrote in second grade. One is a Vietnam War saga, whose main character is a thinly disguised version of my brother, a newly inducted marine, and concerns what I imagined of his gory heroics. The other is the tale of a rocket ship lost in space, whose astronaut-hero is a thinly disguised version of what I hoped to be someday. Each of these novels is unfinished and is only twenty or so pages, and both are written in blue ink on wide-ruled binder paper. Literary quality aside, these novels are long stretches of writing for a second grader, and most importantly, they were not school assignments.

In retrospect, of course, that second-grade year might seem a moment of prophetic inspiration, prompting a straight line from those early novels to the fiction I began to write in high school and have yet to stop, a destiny commenced. But the invention of those second-grade novels was a much more average and common moment. Maddy, who has made it clear she will not be a writer—much to our relief—wrote several "books" just after she learned to read and write, as did most of her friends. It's a simple thing, really. School teaches you a skill, and in that first excitement, you put it to use, even when the teacher isn't making you.

During that garage excavation my mother also found my second-grade report card. In Miss Cleveland's graceful cursive is an assessment that would become standard on my report cards for years: "A capable student, if he would only apply himself." I was both capable and easily distracted, and therefore utterly average. I learned the skills and put them to use, but had a thousand other things to do—riding bikes, playing army, watching TV. It would be many years before I took up writing fiction again, and it would be another teacher in another school who would lead me to that path. But the most basic skills I would need then were already in place when that muse struck—I could read and write. School did not predict which path I'd follow, but nonetheless readied me for it.

At the bottom of Miss Cleveland's comments there is this final note: "Lewis needs to work on his writing."

Miss Cleveland, it took a long while for your message to get through, but I have been working on my writing for forty years now.

Near the end of fourth grade, I began to wear prescription eyeglasses. It turned out that over the previous summer I had grown as nearsighted as you could get.

I could read books fine, but the blackboard, which had always been clear, was now a blur, and because the rows in which we sat were arranged alphabetically, I sat at the back of the first row, behind my best friend, Jim Bryant, as far from the blackboard as possible.

So after an early conference with my fourth-grade teacher, Miss Babb, where my falling math scores aroused concern, my parents had my eyes tested. With a logic only a child can follow, I had assumed that being unable to see the blackboard this year was some character flaw, and so there was relief in that diagnosis.

But I was mortified at the thought of wearing glasses. We might call them spectacles for a reason; suddenly a "four eyes," I would become a playground spectacle, or so I thought, back when wearing glasses to school could still be a catalyst for taunting. Happily, when Maddy got her glasses, in fifth grade, it was considered a mark of cool among her classmates, a fashion statement.

On the first day I took my glasses to school, I snuck them from my jacket pocket when Miss Babb approached the board, and found I could once again read what was written there. Not only did I find the current lesson on the board—the chief activities at California missions—but I was surprised to discover many new things: the date, our reading assignments, vocabulary words, a list of classroom chores, a hive of information. My math grades quickly rebounded, at least for a while.

I did take some minor teasing for my new accessory, but this only lasted a few days, until some other object of vulnerability presented itself to the playground mob.

In the end, the teasing wouldn't have stopped me; I began wearing my glasses all the time, not just for seeing what was written on the board. It was good to see clearly, I discovered, good to know there were individual leaves on the trees.

Like kindergarten, the blackboard is a recent innovation. Erasable slates, a cheap but durable substitute for costly paper and ink, had been in use for centuries. Students could practice reading and writing and math on their slates, in the classroom or at home. But it wasn't until 1800 that James Pillans, headmaster of the Old High School of Edinburgh, wanting to offer geography lessons to his students that required larger maps, connected a number of smaller slates into a single grand field. And in 1801, George Baron, a West Point mathematics teacher, also began to use a board of connected slates, the most effective way, he found, to illustrate complex formulas to a larger audience.

Although the term *blackboard* did not appear until 1815, the use of these cobbled-together slates spread quickly; by 1809, every public school in Philadelphia was using them. Teachers now had a flexible and versatile visual aid, a device that was both textbook and blank page, as well as a laboratory, and most importantly, a point of focus. The blackboard illustrates and is illustrated. Students no longer simply listened to the teacher; they had reason to look up from their desks.

Like many of the best tools, the blackboard is a simple machine, and in the nineteenth century, in rural areas particularly, it was often made from scratch, rough pine boards nailed together and covered with a mixture of egg whites and the carbon leavings from charred potatoes. By 1840 blackboards were manufactured commercially, smoothly planed wooden boards coated with a thick, porcelain-based paint. In the twentieth century, blackboards were mostly porcelain-enameled steel and could last ten to twenty years. Imagine that, a classroom machine so durable and flexible. In my daughter's schools, computers, scads of them, are replaced every two to three years.

While black was long the traditional color for blackboards, a green porcelain surface, first used around 1930, cut down on glare, and as this green surface became more common, the word *chalkboard* came into use.

Chalk, of course, predates the blackboard. The chalk with which we write on boards isn't actual chalk but gypsum, the dihydrate form of calcium sulfate. Gypsum is found naturally and can be used straight out of the ground in big chunks, but it can also be pulverized, colored, and then compressed into cylinders. My most important high school teacher, Mrs. Jouthas, used a variety of neon-colored chalk to help us differentiate the parts of speech, or follow the rhythms of a Mark Twain paragraph. Mrs. Jouthas's handwriting was compact and immaculate, and she took great pride in her board work, a skill she'd clearly honed over many years and which spoke of her own school's rigorous penmanship instruction.

The last time I saw a real blackboard in a classroom

was during a visit to a still-functioning one-room schoolhouse near Hollister, California. The blackboard had been faithfully reconstructed as a souvenir of the school's past, while the teacher and students mainly used the whiteboards that covered the other walls. Whiteboards are the rule these days, and all to the better, it seems, if only for their lack of screeching. But the whiteboard disallows a long-standing classroom rite: cleaning the erasers.

Slates and chalkboards were often cleaned with dry rags, and no doubt sleeves, but in the late nineteenth century, erasers were developed for this task, blocks of wood (later pressed cardboard) covered with tufted felt, usually black or gray. These erasers needed regular cleaning to knock loose all that chalk crammed into the felt's pores, and while it was occasionally a punishment to clean the erasers, it was most often, at my school, a privilege. Often it was the student with the highest score on a test who was invited to pound two erasers together, happy in a billowing cloud of quite possibly lung-damaging dust.

Another aspect of this privilege was cleaning the blackboard itself, wiping it with a slightly damp rag to a chalkless sheen, making it once again a tabula rasa. But the real joy rested with the erasers, the unalloyed childhood love of making a sanctioned mess, as well as permission to hit things together really hard. But I cannot overlook the "teacher's pet" factor. When I was asked to clean Miss Babb's erasers, it was for *her* that I did so. Everyone else would have left for the day, Miss

Babb would be grading papers at her desk, and I would
be standing just outside the classroom door, thwock-
ing the erasers together, teacher and student working
in concert somehow, me watching the words and numbers and ideas from the previous week as they drifted
out over the playground.

Miss Babb's classroom was arranged in the classic manner: a grid of desks aimed at the blackboard. In fifth
grade, Mr. Addington modified his classroom scheme
by arranging the desks in a chevron design; he split
the class in half and angled the rows of desks toward
one another in open Vs. But we all still faced the blackboard; his innovation only reinforced tradition.

When I visit elementary schools today, I find that the
classic grid is rarely used. Instead, there is a seemingly
endless variety of classroom arrangement, but pods of
four desks facing one another and laid out in a pinwheel
design seems to be the most popular alternative.

The classic grid is often called, rather pejoratively,
"the sage on the stage" or "chalk and talk." The disdain
lurking in these descriptions implies that such a design
puts the teacher first and somehow threatens the students' opportunities for more intimate, self-governed
learning. It's true that in the pods-and-pinwheel design students can more easily work in smaller groups,
but such pods, of course, also offer more opportunity
for subterfuge and mutiny. Still, when I visit a classroom
to present my "what do writers really do" dog-and-pony

show, the chairs in those pods all turn to watch me, and I'm always in front of a whiteboard.

The blackboard-centered classroom offers more than pedagogical efficiency; it also offers an effective set of teaching possibilities. In such a classroom students are focused on the teacher (on a good day), but most importantly, they are focused. The teacher is not the focus of the class but rather a lens through which the lesson is created and clarified. The teacher draws the class toward her, but she projects the lessons onto the blackboard behind her, a blank surface upon which smaller ideas may be gathered into larger ones. The blackboard is the surface of thought.

At Maddy's middle school, Smart Boards are now front and center, and on these interactive whiteboards, she and her fellow scholars and their teachers can connect to the Internet and display bits and pieces of information, work out problems and ideas, annotate and edit their work, shuffle digital objects spatially in order to find new connections. The Smart Board is futuristic, yet it serves the same purpose as the blackboard of my childhood. It gives the student more than something to look at; it provides a necessary focus.

In fourth grade, when Miss Babb led us through the history of the California missions, she not only gave us the facts, she also helped create, on the blackboard in front of us, a group mind, a focused highway of thinking, and one that led us—because it was all of us thinking together—to ideas beyond those in our textbooks.

Arriving at school one morning, we found the names and dates of all twenty-one missions written on the board's right side. In the middle of the board, Miss Babb had drawn a map of California, and once we were calmed and the Pledge of Allegiance said, she led us on a guided tour of the missions. Starting with the earliest and southernmost, San Diego de Alcalá, she traced the trail of missions up the state, year by year, embroidering each stop with stories of the missionaries, soldiers, and native people who forged that seminal piece of California history.

But where did they come from, these missionaries? she asked us. Spain, we all answered, and instantly she erased the map of California, and drew a rough but quick map of the Americas, the Atlantic, and Western Europe. From here, she led us backward in time, down Mexico into South America, a continent we'd studied in Mrs. Bowman's class the year before; each of us in Miss Babb's classroom that day was able to add one fact or another to the story of the continent. From South America, she drew us back to Spain, to Columbus and the beginning of the Age of Exploration. The blackboard is linear and simultaneous.

With another swipe of her eraser, we were back in California, and Miss Babb asked us to name something in our own lives that related directly to the Spanish conquest of the state. This was an easy question. We answered quickly, and each answer was hastily, though primly, written on the board. Mission San Jose—which we would visit as a class in a few weeks. San Jose itself,

the name. Oh, good, Miss Babb said, more names: El
Camino Real, Santa Clara, San Francisco, Santa Cruz,
Monterey, Salinas: all Spanish names. "Tacos," someone
called, and we all laughed, but it was true so it went on
the board, too, and from there, a litany of the Mexican
foods we knew. Someone said, "my grandmother";
someone else said, "my father." Miss Babb drew arrows
from the place-names to the foods to the people; she
connected everything. At such moments, she was not
so much our teacher as our translator.

During science lessons, when Miss Babb drew the solar
system or the structure of a molecule on the blackboard,
my mind became inflamed with new ways of seeing the
universe. The school provided, of course, a science textbook, with lovely illustrations and photographs, some
in color, and detailed descriptions in prose, of the very
same things Miss Babb drew on the board. But it was
not the textbooks that made science infiltrate my brain;
it was Miss Babb and a piece of chalk, her writing on a
blank field. With her there, describing the shape of an
orbit as she drew it, or clicking the chalk on an atom's
nucleus and saying "nucleus" at the same time so we
were sure not to miss it, she brought science to life for
me in a way a textbook could not have.

There is a theatrical element to teaching, and it is
necessary. The physical dramatics of the classroom—
all those bodies and brains ritually focused—can create
a new and singular mind, and foster in the individual
student an urgent hunger to learn. A good teacher, like

Miss Babb, can, with a nod or a wink, or by simply repeating a key phrase slowly and with certain emphasis,
maybe leaning toward her student body, deliver a chapter's worth of information instantly and unforgettably.
Otherwise, we might as well stay home and read to
ourselves. The teacher commands her audience, con-
ducts them.

As had happened in second grade with reading and
writing, when I wrote those early novels, the new scientific concepts to which I was introduced in fourth grade
made me seek out more than school first demanded.

I suddenly begged my parents for a telescope and a
microscope and a chemistry set, and they obliged, one
piece of equipment at a time, as they could afford it.
Though neither my mother nor father had gone to
college—my father never made it to high school—they
knew the value of schooling for their children, or at
least trusted in it. They made sure I did my homework
assignments, helped me with them when I asked, and
talked with me each night, curious about the subjects
I was studying, tying these discussions, when possible,
to the stories we saw on the nightly news. They also
came to school when needed, my mother to help with
snacks and decorations for holiday celebrations, and
my father when it was Career Day, a day on which he
every year thrilled my classmates with tales of being a
navy deep-sea diver. Perhaps most essentially, my parents verified that I went to school every day, as simple
as that. There was little pressure to get perfect grades
or high test scores; school, my parents always told me,

wasn't about competition, it was about learning, and the luxury of being able to acquire knowledge. When I finally did get a telescope, my mother, father, and I stood in the front yard together and gazed upward.

I brought school home with me, "study" being merely an intense form of play, and I was not alone. Jim Bryant and I set up a chemistry lab in his garage, where we conducted infamously dangerous experiments with gasoline; we spent summer nights in a nearby park counting asteroids, and once re-created an entire three-day Gemini space mission in my bedroom. Later Mark Boyer and Mike Avina would join us in our Mad Scientists' Club, as it was officially called. School offered all of us new skills and new vistas, and we felt compelled to put them to use: average students from an average classroom.

Let me be clear, though, on what I mean by average. It's not intended as some false humility, hardly. I use "average," at least when describing myself, with a certain pride and a definite gratitude. I was average in the best ways, and fortunate to be so. I came from a secure and balanced home, and while my parents supported me in school, they did not crush me with their own expectations. I attended a good public school, one that was well maintained and well stocked with supplies, and I was guided by teachers dedicated to their art. I was capable of learning some very complicated lessons, but I was also happily distracted by the millions of things that can, and should, distract all children. Fortunately average.

Being average was no impediment; standing before the blackboard, Miss Babb taught all twenty of us.
She tapped with her chalk on a ragged illustration of
the Milky Way, and let us know that, no matter how
average we might be, grand things waited for us. We
were looking at the blackboard but gazing far beyond
it, led by a piece of chalk and the hand that held it.

As a teacher, I have never been a gifted board worker;
Miss Babb and Mrs. Jouthas, while they might be happy
to know I'm a teacher, would be ashamed of my chalk
skills. I don't have the patience for color coding, and
my handwriting, I see when I step back, is practically
illegible. My "the" frequently looks like "tle." I attack
the board, I don't write on it. And the thing is, I don't
really need to use the board at all. My graduate writing
classes are small seminars with rarely more than ten
students. We sit around a large table (or smaller tables
smooshed together) and we talk. We read from books,
we read from manuscripts, we suffer through small si-
lences, but mostly we talk. The ideas build up in the air
above our heads.

But every once in a while I can't help myself and
have to go to the whiteboard. I scribble on it and draw
pictures, try to "illustrate" my points. In an early class
discussion on the history of the novel, I frequently
bring up Stendhal's phrase "the mirror in the roadway,"
which the critic Frank O'Connor uses to describe the
form of the novel. For me this phrase is key to understanding that a novel is about the journey of its charac-

ters, but a journey that is also a reflection of the world through which the characters pass. The mirror in the roadway is a strange but effective metaphor, yet I cannot do it justice with words alone. So I get up and draw a roadway, and a mirror in that roadway, and moving toward that mirror, a wagonload of characters. I'm not a draftsman, and unless I tell you what I'm drawing on the board, you would never know there was a horse-drawn wagon, much less a mirror or a roadway.

Once I start on the board, I often can't stop and continue to add phrases, strange pictures, the titles of books, sometimes just marks, a kind of visual punctuation. The ham of my left hand will be covered with red or blue or green dry-erase marker by the end of the evening, and when I stand back to look over what I've written, nothing makes any sense. My board work looks more like a foreign language than literary criticism. But it's still effective board work. I've been able to draw connections; I've been able to drive home key points. I've made the students look beyond me, themselves, and our little room.

As terrifying as it can be, there is value in the student being told to go to the board alone. Removed from one's desk, that all-too-comfortable zone, the student is put in a new relation to the rest of the class.

The clichéd image of a child alone at a blackboard is seen each week during the opening credits of *The Simpsons,* when Bart writes his lines, repeating one sentence a hundred times, punishment for his high jinks.

I saw nothing unusual in the teacher's lounge.
WWII could not beat up WWI.
Teachers' unions are not ruining this country.
Blackboarding is not a form of torture.
We DO need no education.

Bart has lovely board skills, and his printing is immaculate. I suspect, however, that this form of punishment is long gone and exists only in nostalgia.

Bart's is a solitary punishment, suffered alone after school. The real terror, for me at least, in standing before the blackboard, came during class, when I might be called on to "show my work." At such moments, the student is completely vulnerable—to public failure, to private anxieties, to an absolute freeze on all thought. School, by its nature, is filled with moments of terror—as is any journey into the wider world. But that terror is mitigated, to a degree, by the security and order of the classroom. School can, in its best forms, allow us to move beyond our terror.

I recall a precise moment of blackboard terror in Miss Babb's fourth grade, one I may never forget, and of course, it involved math. It was a silver-bright afternoon, and I was directed to the blackboard to solve an equation as part of a contest, the left half of the class versus the right. I was not the first contestant that day, and so I knew there was a chance of *not* failing; some of the equations were long division, my nemesis, but some were multiplication, in which I was fluent. *Please, God,* I silently prayed, *or whoever is in charge of math, please let it be multiplication.*

I stood at the board, chalk ready, and sensed my classmates waiting gleefully for me to fail in a gossip-worthy manner. As with most spectator sports, failure is often the more alluring outcome.

Miss Babb called out the first number—I don't re-call the exact number, but it was four digits long—and my hope rose. But then she called out the function, "divided by," followed by a three-digit number. Not just long division: impossible long division. A collec-tive gasp filled the room. I wrote down the numbers, put the larger one in the half house that is the division symbol, the smaller number knocking at the door like a hungry wolf.

I was okay through the first column of division, but during the next, I saw that I had already screwed up. I motored on, though, as if stubbornness would win out. Growing desperate, and wishing only to be finished now, I faked the ending. I looked to Miss Babb: was I even close?

"That is incorrect," she said, ticking her score sheet.

Titters all around.

Miss Babb joined me at the board, and we worked out the problem together. I had transposed two num-bers—a tic of mine, one my daughter shares—and all that followed was therefore wrong. Miss Babb asked me to find the transposition and I did; I swiped the board with my fist for an eraser and was back on track. Then she showed me that the columns of numbers, which fell out of the equation like gnarled roots, had gotten con-fused, and I had moved over one column where I hadn't intended to. Some vertical lines, she showed, would keep the columns sorted for me. I erased everything but the equation, put in the columns, and started over. I got it right this time: half a point. Errors were made, but I had not failed.

From behind me, I heard a collective sigh of relief. While my fellow students were at first thrilled by my "failure," they also knew their turn was coming, and were relieved, it seemed, that the contest was not lost yet. Math wasn't black magic, and there was hope for us all.

The blackboard is a wonderful place to make a mistake. It's not permanent, and a mistake here can be righted immediately. Not only did Miss Babb show me where I went wrong, but everyone else in the class could see my error and learn from it. I no longer felt alone. On a blackboard, redemption is possible.

To stand before a class like this is a lot of pressure on a kid. But it offers an important lesson, one of those larger lessons that school gives us, whether we like it or not. School wants to put us in unique situations, frightening ones sometimes, and to be able to perform in front of others is a valuable skill. To be able to make a mistake and then rectify it with critical thinking is a basic strategy with far-reaching implications. School drags us, sometimes kicking and screaming, out of our shells.

I surely would have been more comfortable that day if I had been allowed to stay at my desk, but I would have remained baffled by long division. That terrifying moment in front of the blackboard changed me, and for the good.

The Life of the Classroom

The life of the classroom, I'm reminded while visiting Bagby, isn't always about education. There's an entire other life that unfolds at school, one that ignores textbooks, quizzes, blackboards, teachers. The student is not a visitor here, neither client nor consumer; school is where the student lives her life.

When I pick up Maddy at the end of the day, I always ask, "How was school?" "Good," she says, the end of the conversation, although now and then I get a fuller report: a difficult or "unfair" test, a prank pulled on a teacher, maybe a tidbit of what Maddy calls "drama-drama," the agonizing shifts in boy/girl alliances. I'm happy enough with her shorthand answer; after all, she's been at school all day and is ready, for the moment, to think about something else. We turn up the radio and head home, watching the fog tumble in over Twin Peaks.

Though I'm often frustrated with "good" and would really like a fuller report, I remember that I frequently answered my parents in a similar vein, guarding my inner life, as Maddy must guard hers when she needs to. I've also come to realize that my question to her is as much shorthand as her answer. How could she possibly tell me all that happened at school that day? School comprises more than what was "covered," what homework needs to be completed, how those grades are coming along.

At Maddy's current school, I volunteer in the library a few Wednesdays each month, where I help giddy second graders find books on hamsters and *Star Wars*, by far, library records show, their two favorite subjects. Maddy is clear she prefers not to see me on these days, and I would have said the same to my parents once: what eighth grader wants to find his parents at school? But San Francisco Friends is a small school, and now and then, I do spot her, tripping down the hall with friends, laughing and conspiratorial. Or there she is at her lab table in science class, and though she seems to be paying attention, I suspect she's daydreaming. Or in an otherwise empty corridor, she sits on the floor, rushing through workbook assignments. School is not her day, it is her life, whether she likes it or not.

Time is different for kids. Maddy's school day is a sprint for me, and after I drop her off in the morning, I have to hustle head-down to get through my list of chores before 3:15 arrives. But for Maddy, those seven hours move in ways I fear I've forgotten; her hours flow in waves and pulses, stopping and starting, and an awful lot transpires within those currents. By the end of Maddy's eighth-grade day, she's been to six classes and enjoyed two recesses and a long lunch. She's taken tests, corrected homework, read entire chapters of novels, sung with a chorus, rehearsed a scene from Shakespeare, played volleyball, worked on her high school applications.

Then there's her social life. How much time has she spent chatting with friends? Threads of communication crisscross her day: notes are passed back and forth, electronic and otherwise; likes and dislikes are revealed and concealed. Entire social structures—who is in and who is out, what is cool and what is now passé—may change completely, then reverse again, all between the first and last bells.

I cannot recall a single classroom of my own, from kindergarten through high school, that did not have a round, white-faced clock above the blackboard. Year after year, I stared at those clocks, learning lessons about the nature of time, how it is anything but standard.

As an elementary student, when I was fully involved in a pleasurable task—I'm thinking in particular of holiday art projects: Halloween pumpkins, Christmas wreaths, Valentine hearts, Easter baskets—an hour might bound nimbly across the white spaces of the day. "Time's up," the teacher would say, deflating us all. Or if I were taking a test, the end of the allotted half hour might appear suddenly next to my desk, tapping an impatient finger: pencils down.

Time might as easily begin to crawl, too, congeal

into its molasses state. In the early mornings, when it seemed we had been working and working, wandering toward yet another California mission, like those weary Spanish soldiers on their underfed horses, I might look up to find first recess still half an hour distant, and that thirty minutes might loiter on the spot for days.

But it was at the end of the day that time played its most dastardly tricks. The minute hands of Bagby's clocks did not progress gradually but discretely, clicking audibly to the next minute only when the second hand had mowed through the round field of time. *Click,* a rush to the next minute, followed by patient hours of waiting for the succeeding minute to arrive. At five minutes to three, with everyone, including the teacher, sleepy and oh so ready to leave, nothing left to say, not an ounce of brain among us, the clock might simply stop. A day could go by: *cah-lick.* Another day, maybe two: *cah-lick.* I would urge the clock forward, rage and rail, but nothing. And to compound my frustration, the minute hands of Bagby's clocks actually leaned back a bit before clicking to the next station, as if gathering momentum. The clock took its own sweet time, taught me exasperating lessons in relativity, in torpor and endurance. Until—ring! The last bell.

Between the clicks of the minute hands, the winding rivers of hours, the loud but always welcome bells, that's where the student lives. *Four seasons in one day.*

Having attended a French immersion lower school, and now a Quaker middle school, Maddy has never had to recite the Pledge of Allegiance. But most American public school days begin with this inescapable ritual.

Facing the flag, we put our hands over our hearts. When my mother was a child, students saluted the flag with right arm extended and elevated, palm down, a salute appropriated by the Nazis. American schoolchildren used this salute until 1942, when President Franklin D. Roosevelt changed it by law and introduced "hand over heart." There must have been an effective campaign of forgetting that followed; it's difficult to find classroom photos of the earlier salute.

Hands over hearts, composed and quiet, my classmates and I recited the pledge.

> *I pledge allegiance to the Flag of the United States of America, and to the Republic for which it stands, one Nation under God, indivisible, with liberty and justice for all.*

I didn't set out to type the pledge right here, but like the alphabet, and the times tables, it is etched into my memory whole. I said these words so often and so ritualistically that when I started typing today, I had to finish.

The pledge was more than a patriotic mantra. Fresh from the morning playground's hustle and bustle, we stepped into a quieter place and breathed the same words into the same air. By its very habit, *every single day*, we lost the sense of the pledge's words but not their effect: a quickly muttered prayer, a long deep breath, a bow to the four quarters.

Once the pledge was recited, we slid into our desks, ready to commence our first lessons.

My desk was my command center, vantage point, launching pad, warehouse, retreat. It was where I spent a good part of my day for most of the days of my school years, and although I had different desks in elementary school, one each year, they all remained the singular *my desk*. This was where I arranged and categorized the world, where I followed the ebb and flow of the life of the classroom, and where I kept the hoard of everything I held valuable.

Visiting a fifth-grade classroom at Bagby today, I approach a student, who, after a scrupulous appraisal of this stranger, agrees to let me catalog his desk. I don't blame his suspicion; I'm being a snoop. When he opens his desk, there is his whole life: textbooks, Yu-Gi-Oh! cards, wadded-up homework assignments, indecipherable junk, candy wrappers, a storm-flattened forest of stuff. The girl next to him, not wanting to be left out, shows me her desk, which is, no surprise, neatly arranged into tidy work spaces and play areas. It is also decorated with stickers and pictures from magazines that are attached to the inside of the lid. I shared this impulse; on the inside of my desk lid, I once taped pictures of the Lovin' Spoonful and Herman's Hermits, movie ads for *Planet of the Apes, Goldfinger, Fantastic Voyage,* and my own drawings of tanks and airplanes.

In American classrooms before the Civil War, when the majority of students attended one-room schoolhouses, contiguous tables were the standard, each table affixed to a wall. Seated at these tables on communal benches, students faced the wall while working on their own, then spun around to follow group lessons. Tables and benches were much cheaper than stand-alone desks, and the local handyman might bang them together.

Along one wall, the teacher had his own desk—before the Civil War the majority of teachers were men—often on a raised platform. In a one-room school-house, this configuration was one not merely of economy but also of flexibility. These buildings were what we might call today multipurpose rooms: community meeting places, churches, recreation halls, occasionally a fortress against Indian raids. Individual desks took up too much room.

But after the Civil War, when larger and more centralized schools were constructed, schools funded by broader tax bases, the classroom could be dedicated to the single purpose of teaching. Yet in spite of more abundant public funding, up through the 1920s stand-alone desks were almost always bolted to the floor.

Consider the mythological desk, the Ur-desk, the one of cartoon and caricature. It has a black-painted, wrought-iron base that is decoratively curlicued, and attached to this base, sometimes on a swivel, is a wood-slatted seat. The desktop is a hinged wooden lid, while the bowl of the desk may be wood or iron. In the surface of the desk, farthest from the student, is a trough for pencil or pen, and a shallow divot for an inkwell. It is into this inkwell, cartoons insist, that many pigtails are dipped. The lid of this desk is tattooed with designs:

jackknife carved initials, romances and curses, and of
course, warnings—*Property of*...

My elementary school desk was essentially no different from the mythological one. The swivel seat still
attached to the base, but this base was made of stainless
steel, a design more atomic-age sleek than Victorian
ornamental, a one-piece tripod that might have served
as a launchpad for rockets to Mars. The lid of my desk
was meant to resemble blond wood, though it was
rather pink in hue and had never been close to wood.
Its faux-grain surface was protected by a slick layer of
transparent laminate, the better for cleaning, and for
arresting, though not quite halting, graffiti. The inkwell was missing, but the pen trough remained, both
vestigial and practical; the trough kept pens and pencils
from rolling away. The bowl of the desk, painted gray,
was infinitely capacious, a prosperously midcentury
American space, a two-car garage of a desk, holding
anything and everything.

Through junior high school, high school, and college, the shapes of my desk changed, as I began to carry
my books and supplies from room to room. These
desks were less welcoming: *You'll only be here for fifty
minutes, so don't get comfortable.* In junior high and high
school, the desks were mostly flat surfaces, sans bowls,
with a wire rack under the seat to hold the books for my
next class. In college, there were chairs with convert-
ible tabletops, oddly shaped, that covered only half of
my lap but that could be lowered to the side with a flip
of the wrist. These were my least-favorite desks; they

are made for right-handed students, but since I'm a lefty I had to twist and slouch to take notes there.

A few weeks after my visit to Bagby, I made a similar pilgrimage to my old high school, and the desks were much larger than I remembered. The classroom, though, in contrast to my kindergarten, seemed quite a bit smaller. I thought that perspective and age were playing tricks on me again, until Branham's vice-principal explained that, because of the obesity epidemic, high school desks today were considerably larger. I wasn't seeing things; the space in the classroom really was smaller, more crowded.

There was one serious design flaw in my elementary school desk, at least from the teacher's point of view. From the student's point of view, this flaw was a boon, one that made possible much of my nonschool school life. Because the lid of my desk opened nearest me, when I lifted the lid, the teacher could not see me. The lid was as wide as the desk itself, and I was quite small, and behind this slab of plastic, I could hide in the world that was my desk.

The one thing I did not keep in my desk, and wisely so, was my lunch box. Lunch boxes were stashed with our jackets near the back of the room; in the 1960s there were no plastic seals or thermal insulation to suppress the odors of warm milk, waxed-paper-wrapped tuna sandwiches, or ripe bananas. Happily for me, the 1960s was the golden age of the metal lunch box, and I went through at least one a year: Daniel Boone, Lost in Space,

G.I. Joe, Gomer Pyle. Only a few years later, a swift yet irrational fear of playground fights and paralyzing brain injuries outlawed, if only briefly, metal lunch boxes, though it's clear now such fears were ungrounded.

Lunch boxes excepted, I kept everything else in my desk. Workbooks and readers, science and history and math texts. A denim-covered three-hole binder and a plastic-wrapped mini-ream of extra paper. Manila-colored *Pee Chee* folders—technically *Pee Chee All Season Portfolios*—with stylized drawings of high school athletes on their covers, and on the inside pockets, charts of what were deemed useful data: the multiplication table; a metric conversion chart; durations of time; dry weights and liquid volumes; linear, circular, surface, and cubic measurements; avoirdupois, troy, and apothecary weights (did you know that twenty grains equals one scruple?).

A few yellow number 2 pencils, cheap ballpoint pens, pink trapezoidal erasers, a wooden ruler with an inset metal edge, a compass and a protractor, all kept in a plastic zippered pouch, what French schoolchildren call a *trousse,* as in *trousseau.* I also kept for several years a collection of neon-hued mechanical pencils that I never used—my hand was too Neanderthal for their delicate leads—but which I felt the need to own anyway.

I always had a small pencil sharpener in my desk, plastic with a little bubble for the shavings, but I rarely used it. I much preferred the industrial-strength, brown-and-gray metal wall-mounted sharpener near the teacher's desk. The advantage of using the "big" pencil sharpener was that I got to get up from my desk. I loved cranking the handle, feeling the lead and wood surrender to the geared teeth, and changing the bore for no reason—there must have been eight different bores on those Boston-brand sharpeners, but were there really that many sizes of pencil? Then, whether it needed to be done or not, I would empty the shavings into the trash for that fresh, heaped smell of wood and graphite, a little pillow of aroma released into the day.

Nonschool items, however, probably took up most of my desk space, with an emphasis on candy: Necco wafers, Chuckles, Good & Plenty, Pixie Stix straws, SweetTarts, Pell Mell candy cigarettes, bubble gum cigars, Tootsie-Pops. I snuck bites of candy during class, and traded candies clandestinely while the teacher's back was turned.

I also kept objects that, if discovered, would be confiscated by the teacher: toys. But it had to be the right kind of toy, one that carried a certain playground cachet. At Bagby, this meant troll dolls. Trolls were (and still are) squat plastic figures with goofy grins and dimpled cheeks, pointy ears, glassy eyes, and pushed-up pig-like noses; they are harshly cute. What most drew us to trolls was their hair. It was real synthetic hair, not molded plastic, and it stood straight up in the shape of a cartoon candle flame. The hair was always a ridiculous color: blue, orange, lime, pink, rainbow. Trolls could be dressed in an allowance-depleting variety of costumes: football player, ballerina, astronaut, hippie, U.S. marine. The standard troll was about three inches high (sans hair), a perfect desk size, easily concealed. If you were anybody at Bagby, you collected trolls.

And yo-yos, tops, Matchbox cars, small sticks, cool-looking rocks, a treasury as plentiful and pretty as a bowerbird's. The stash in my desk was important, in part, because it was under my control, not seen or infiltrated by my parents, nor, I imagined, by the teacher or the school custodian. I believed my desk was inviolable, protected by the Constitution we studied so assiduously.

But the things in one's desk can also be a source of income, as it were, up for trade. When Maddy was in lower school, new toy fads swept through the playground two or three times a year: Peek-a-Poohs, Kooky Pens, Polly Pocket dolls and their accessories; and for the boys, Pokémon cards, miniature robots, action figures from the latest film.

As I had with trolls, Maddy and her friends traded Peek-a-Poohs: one-inch rubber Winnie the Poohs dressed in different costumes. And the trading of these could often be rather ruthless, the girls placing inflated values on some, debasing others, and sometimes making complex three- and four-way deals: A will give B two of Peek-a-Pooh X, if C will trade B Peek-a-Pooh Y with a compensation of Peek-a-Pooh Z going to A at a later date. Barterer's remorse is common in such deals; the lust for one Peek-a-Pooh might result in the hasty, thoughtless trade of another. But the rules are hard and fast: no takebacks. Black markets thrive at schools, and not just in enviable lunches and coveted desserts. Your desk is your warehouse, the playground your trading floor.

For the more adventurous student, a desk can also be a little zoo. I once kept a jar of polliwogs in my desk, to disastrous consequences, and Jim Bryant, and I both brought our pet mice to school, where we nested them in our desks for an entire week, allowing them to visit each other on occasion. That the mice made it back to our homes alive was certainly a miracle.

My desk at school was very much like my room at home, half chaos and half order. I was always tidying it and checking its inventory, while at the same time raiding it for toys and candies, or adding them. And because my inventory was paramount, the messiest sections tended to be homework sheets and textbooks. My desk, like my room, has always been a three-dimensional representation of my brain: part focus and part distraction.

Seated at our desks, those little desert islands, my classmates and I maintained, as best we could, a semblance of order, but never a complete order, never a completely public life. Within the structures of the classroom, there is also the hidden life of school.

I sent my fair share of folded notes across rows and rows, a telegraph of notes that, if interrupted by the teacher, might be read aloud to the class. Cheating on tests with whispered pleas, crib notes up sleeves and in socks or inked on skin. An entire society can exist without the teacher knowing, or at least acknowledging it.

In Mr. Addington's fifth grade, for months that spring, the boys played a long-standing game of Ruler Wars. Because Mr. Addington had arranged the class in a chevron, the rows slanted toward one another, we could, while he wrote on the board, slip our rulers from inside our desks out the crack of the front hinge, each ruler a cannon and each desk a fortress. We fired imaginary cannon balls across the room, with no other rules to the game than imagined explosions and the destruction that might follow. I respected Mr. Addington a good deal— something about his sweaters made him seem "intellec- tual" to me—so this game was not about disrespect.

A few months ago when I picked up Maddy at school, I offered her the usual "how was your day?," expecting the standard "good" but getting instead the rare fuller version. "It was one of those days," she said, "where I just stared out the window. I didn't really pay attention. All those clouds. Did you see the storm? I mostly stared out the window."

Phew. I don't want Maddy's school life to be so single- minded she can't just stare out the window now and then. A recent book on creativity in the workplace makes the case that some of the best business ideas are fostered by daydreaming, and so I can fall back on that defense, though I'm loath to relegate daydreaming to economic efficiency. Sometimes you have to daydream simply be- cause it's a worthwhile endeavor of its own.

Maddy's middle school classrooms are on the third floor of an old Levi's factory, and the view from there is decidedly distracting, across the Mission District to downtown San Francisco and a slim view of the bay beyond. At Bagby, the high windows that lined one wall of each of my classrooms were irresistible—why would you want to resist? I recall one day when I did nothing, it seemed, but watch a willow tree blown by gusty winds, and I never tired of tracking the black rain clouds of the Santa Clara Valley as they consumed spring's blue vault.

Staring out the window is a vital piece of the curriculum. Much work is done there.

Back to Miss Babb's fourth grade. I lift the desk's lid, whisper to Jim Bryant, "Hey, whacha wanna do at recess?" Miss Babb is trying to interest us in the idea of multiplying fractions, but I really can't pay attention to her right now. The clock is about to rear back and hurtle forward, and when that bell rings, Jim and I will fly from our desks out onto the school grounds, where yet more worlds await.

School Grounds

Though I most often loved going to school, there were also days when I hated to, days when I simply could not conceive of getting out of bed, much less walking *all the way* to school and spending the *whole day* there. There is no underlying psychological cause here; this is just the way kids are sometimes, tired and cranky and stubborn—much like adults when it comes to their jobs.

I occasionally tried to feign an illness, but my working mother, who had raised my brother and sister already, knew all those tricks, and when I was truly ill, it was always when I was ill enough that she felt compelled to stay home with me.

By fifth grade, however, I had been introduced to the joy of cutting school—*hooking out,* as Twain would have it. Every once in a while my father faked an illness or a doctor's appointment on my behalf, and we'd spend the day fishing in Watsonville or swimming from the beach in Santa Cruz, learning scuba at one of his navy pals' dive schools, visiting shipyards and steel mills. My father and I had always been very close—"great pals" was what he often told his friends—and those days we spent outside school remain some of my fondest memories. I have not been so kind to my daughter: I make her go to school all the time, but fear the loss is both of ours.

Given my father's example and what I understood to be his tacit permission, I decided one day to play hooky on my own. I walked all the way to school that morning, then returned home and let myself in, knowing that my parents had left for work. It was a long boring day without my father's companionship and car, and a somewhat anxiety-prone one—I assumed I'd get caught out any minute. I mostly watched television. Returning to school the next morning, I proudly handed over my forged absence note, which was written in red ink on a 3- by 5-inch index card: *Dear Mr. Addington, please excuse Lewis from school yesterday. His stomach hurted. Sincerely, Lewis's dad, Mr. Buzbee.* Mr. Addington called my parents that evening, and the punishment came down, swift but not too furious: I was grounded for two weeks, a sentence difficult to enforce on a latchkey kid. My parents seemed more amused by my trespass than angry. Still I did not play hooky again until my first two years of high school, when my life and circumstances greatly altered, and truancy became something of a habit.

But in elementary school, no matter how much I hated the idea of sitting in a classroom for the entire day, there was always the fact of recess, and that fact was often enough to get me out the door on a sullen morn-

ing. Recess, it seemed to me then, was the first intent of
school, the teachers and classes and homework merely
the outline that gave recess its bright and alluring shape.
And standing on Bagby's asphalt playground today, it's
clear this school was built for recess. School grounds,
their buildings and play yards, are a reflection of what
the school intends for its students, and those who designed and built Bagby clearly wanted us to run and
play. Bagby was a large and self-sufficient planet, whose
buildings and fields were solely created, it seemed, for
me and my exploration of them. I was meant to own
and inhabit the entirety of these school grounds—this
was *my* school.

Bagby Elementary was built in 1956, at the height of
the post–World War II economic and population boom
that blanketed California's Santa Clara Valley, and large
swaths of the United States, with subdivisions, shopping
centers, and of course, schools. Like most school buildings, Bagby's mirrored the community's own architectural style.

In 1962, just before my kindergarten year, our family
moved into a modest but nearly brand-new ranch home
in a subdivision surrounded by other new subdivisions,
miles and miles of look-alike homes. It took me many
years to understand why my mother chose to paint our
house a motel-pool shade of turquoise, but it was a fairly
obvious strategy: we would always be able to locate our
glowing house among the dowdier beiges and pastels.

Until the 1950s, this flat section of the western valley
was nothing but fruit orchards, cherry and plum and
apricot, and until I was in second grade, there was still
a cherry orchard at the end of our block; we raided its
fruit early every spring. California was just over one
hundred years old as a state at the time, and this was
fresh land, with a hint of the frontier still in the air, or
so the common mythology told us, the untamed West.
Frank Lloyd Wright's approach to architecture, that it
be organic, of the culture and the landscape in which
it was set, had by then filtered down to the more ple-
beian levels of building, and since this was the West,
ranch houses were required.

Ours was an L-shaped, three-bedroom ranch, of no
particular remark in its interiors. Architecturally what
made it a ranch house were the peaked but gently sloped
roofline and the broad eaves that shaded the windows
against the intense California sun. Dark, wooden, and
fire-prone shingles squashed the house's profile; our
house hugged the ground, huddled there on the new
frontier. The wood trim on our stucco house was laid
in geometric designs that were vaguely cowboy-ish, as
if you might make a branding iron of them.

But the hallmark of the ranch home was the lawn.
Our lot was quite small, and the backyard rather
cramped, but, oh, the front lawn, a vast, unbroken prai-
rie of Kentucky bluegrass that needed far too much wa-
tering in California's drought-prone semidesert climate.
It was a lawn that took days to mow, a lawn on which

football games could be played, and with room enough for a herd of cattle and the horses necessary to round them up.

Bagby Elementary is itself a grand sprawling ranch house; it has the gently sloped roofline and broad, low eaves of the houses that surround it. Two parallel rows of classrooms form the base of an L, from the kindergarten to the cafetorium, with a single row of classrooms for the longer side; it is a footprint identical to the house I grew up in. The buildings are stucco with minor wooden trim, too, though the fire-thirsty shingles were replaced by a much safer tar and gravel roof. The classrooms, one next to the other, each with separate doors, mimicked the arrangement of the bedrooms in our house.

What distinguishes Bagby from most prewar schools is that the entrances to both the school and the classrooms are all exterior; classroom doors open directly onto open-air walkways, beyond which are, immediately, the play structures and playing fields that were our own little kingdoms, and when it was time for recess or lunch or going home, I just had to walk out the door and was already where I wanted to be, *outside*.

The design of these open-air schools was, in part, dictated by building costs, which could be minimized thanks to the weather. This part of California is so temperate and arid that interior hallways were not necessary; students were not going to freeze going from class to class, nor were they going to track snow in on their boots. At worst, we might get a little rain blown in the spring. Bagby's was a simple design, one suited to its terrain.

As an unfortunate reflection of how the world has changed since Bagby was built, open-air designs are used less frequently today, even in soft-weather regions like California. The open-air footprint, because of its many entrances and exits, is difficult to secure against truancy, graffiti, vandalism, and the more violent school invasions. While metal detectors, barred windows, locked gates, and sometimes armed guards may seem necessary at some schools, such safeguards also send a disquieting message to students who pass through these gauntlets. Students already feel vulnerable at school—in the public sphere, away from home—but the best schools by their very nature mitigate that vulnerability. The safeguards of a locked-down school announce that it is a dangerous place. A school needs to welcome its students, not screen them.

This fall, scouting high schools for Maddy, we visited several San Francisco Unified School District campuses. A few of the campuses are lovely, but many are decrepit. One school, with a deserved reputation for its academic programs, was so dismal—peeling paint, dirty and cracked windows, classrooms in windowless basements, and a pervasive dilapidation—that our family could not even consider the school's educational assets. Through no fault of the school's principal, teachers, students, or parents—that fault lies squarely with insufficient funding from the state of California—this otherwise fine school is undermined by its physical condition.

If we want our children to thrive at school, shouldn't their schools welcome them each day, make them feel as if their school is a place they want, rather than have, to be?

Each of us carries an image of capital-S School, the child's archetypal drawing of what we mean by the word. For me, of course, it's Bagby Elementary, a broad suburban campus surrounded by acres of grassy playing fields.

Maddy, a San Francisco child, has attended decidedly urban schools. Her elementary school, French American International, occupies a six-story former office building that is surrounded by car-choked streets and a neighborhood both a tad grimy and a tad posh. Two small asphalt yards, each with a few rudimentary pieces of playground equipment, are enclosed by chain-link fences and cement walls. Near the main entrance is a cursory patch of lawn where kids eat lunch on sunny days, but for most of the time, FAIS students are squeezed into cacophonous corridors and low-ceilinged classrooms. While the building has its charms, the school clearly emphasizes that the academic life is central here.

Maddy's middle school, San Francisco Friends, is in a livelier but funkier neighborhood—cafés, liquor stores, tattoo parlor, pot club. A wrought-iron fence keeps the students from the street, and the street from the students. But even though Maddy and her pals spend most of their day indoors, SF Friends, being Quaker, is a soft place. The 1906 three-story building was, until 1997, a Levi Strauss jeans factory, and in retrofitting the building, the school's founders retained the high ceilings, broad interior hallways, and brushed wooden floors. There's still clamor here—it is a school, after all—but there's room for echo and silence and hidden spaces. Rather than squeezing in as many classrooms and offices as possible, as was done at French American International, careful, noneconomical choices were made to ensure that the space worked for its students, both in and out of the classroom.

Springfield Elementary on *The Simpsons,* as happens in the best cartoons, portrays a common type, an American school whose portrait is broad enough to illustrate the general, yet specific enough to evoke the particular. The building is two stories, constructed of a peachy-yellow stone, for which you may insert brick or brownstone or concrete or wood, as fitting. Rows of tall windows on both floors mark the classrooms. The design is angularly modern, but hints in its details at a Depression-era style. On the front lawn, located essentially, the American flag naps at the top of an aluminum pole.

A set of steps leads to a single entry, from which long interior corridors lead to classrooms that are traditionally rectangular and gridded with desks. Bart stands, eternally, before the blackboard, writing his lines. When necessary for an episode, Springfield Elementary may contain a gymnasium, a cafeteria complete with hot-lunch line, a principal's office, a teacher's lounge, a library, a bus lane, a faculty parking lot, a basement with a boiler room. The playground is American classic: swings and monkey bars, tetherball and four-square and hopscotch blacktops, and a large fenced-in field.

What did your school grounds say to you? What invitation did it extend? And your child's school grounds?

Recess was certainly not my only longed-for freedom from teachers and desks. There were many other places at school to get away to, important avenues of inquiry through which I made the school mine.

A trip to the "lavatory" was always a ready possibility, a trip drawn out longer than necessary, especially if I chose to dawdle at the drinking fountain, a white porcelain trough at the far end of the classroom wing. Aside from the utilitarian nature of this excursion, and the general respite from class work, a trip to the lavatory offered me a defamiliarized view of my daily world. School was in session, the classrooms teeming with business, but in the hallways I found a deep and abiding quiet, and saw the school as if for the first time, uninterrupted by the chatter and crash of my cohort. The school seemed larger during these trips, possessed of more interesting architectural details—the flying-saucer shape of the overhead lamps, the arrangement of the drain pipes, the welds and rivets of steel posts and beams, the chipped forest-green paint of the wooden benches. During the brittle hush of the Cold War, we were often instructed to imagine life after a nuclear war, and I imagined, as I moseyed toward the lavatory, that postapocalyptic Earth would feel something like this, a deep, still hollow, beautiful in its way.

Other errands could take me out of class, too. A visit to the nurse's office for symptoms, true or willed-to-be-true, offered a peculiar glimpse of school life. While in class, I rarely thought about the administrative life of the school, but in the nurse's office, lying on a paper sheet on a vinyl daybed, a mercury thermometer under my tongue, I could hear the phones ringing, the secretaries chatting, the principal coming and going, parents arriving for conferences. I was always at ease in the nurse's office—rarely ill enough to be uneasy—and marveled at the knowledge that the world continued to spin outside our classrooms.

On occasion, usually on the grounds that I too often "socialized" in class, I was called to the principal's office. It's true, I did socialize a bit much, unable to keep quiet and needing absolutely to talk to Jim Bryant about our Mad Scientist plans for later that day, or to whomever else about another pressing matter. The teacher would ask me a few times to be quiet and pay attention, then she would send a note to the school's office, and I would be summoned by the principal later in the day. At Bagby this summons was public, delivered by loudspeaker; everyone in class knew where I were going: "Lewis Buzbee to the principal's office." This announcement was always followed by a classwide "ooooooooh." Only once, as I recall, was I summoned for a more serious offense, on the day Raymond Aver and I got into a fistfight at recess that ended with a little blood—I had been defending the honor of my third-grade teacher, Mrs. Bowman.

Such a trip, needless to say, was not a leisurely excursion, but a solitary journey down long empty corridors, on my way to certain doom in the principal's darkly paneled office. The eventual punishment never rivaled the expectation, as if the journey was punishment enough.

Another important nonclass space at Bagby was the lunchroom, where we would eat for half an hour, then hightail it outside. Ours was no ordinary lunchroom, mind you; it was a cafetorium, that hybrid of cafeteria and auditorium. Six-inch stainless steel sans serif letters spelled out *Cafetorium* above the double-door entrance—the same letters are there today. Once, in second or third grade, I stopped to stare at this word, suddenly aware that it was a fancy but made-up word created from two other fancy words, a feat that made me feel supremely sophisticated, a genuine self-teaching moment.

At one end of the cafetorium is a small stage, where plays about Pilgrims and missions are performed, where music students recite their recitals, where the principal stands during assemblies, where graduations are held. Along the walls, foldout tables emerge during lunches, and during my tenure, we sat according to grade. Whether this arrangement was by administrative fiat or through natural selection, I don't recall. Grade mixing was always a suspicious activity.

Brown baggers and lunch boxers were allowed to eat outside, but I was about half lunch box, half hot lunch, and on my cafetorium days, I stood in line with a tray, offered one quarter and one dime to the cashier, and moved down the serving line. For my thirty-five cents, I received one hot entrée, two vegetable sides, one dessert-like object, and a half pint of milk that was never cold enough. Lunch ladies in pink rayon dresses and pink hair nets scooped out the meals and moved me along. My favorite entrées: a crater of mashed potatoes filled with hamburger gravy; fat tubular pasta in a red sauce. My favorite vegetables: Tater Tots and lima beans. Dessert: Rice Krispie squares. My least favorite entrée was breaded fish sticks; though ours was not a Catholic school, we always had some form of fish on Fridays.

The hot lunches of my era were afforded by a federally subsidized program that served all public school students, not only those below a certain economic level. That program, intended to ensure a hot lunch for all who wanted it, a verifiable educational advantage, was long ago suspended. At Bagby today, the lunch ladies merely unpack food from caterers' trays that are trucked in every morning. No food is cooked here any longer; it is deemed economically unviable to do so.

The cafetorium is the one place during my visit that seems markedly smaller, and I think it's because I toured it when it was empty. I suspect that if it were filled with children and the hurricane of noise that naturally hovers over them, the cafetorium would seem larger again. Imagine how many plans and conspiracies and alliances form here.

As soon as we were done with lunch, it was dump the tray on the conveyor belt and get down to the serious business of recess.

My favorite space at school, without question, and the aspect of Bagby that most mirrored its community, was the playing field, that enormous front lawn. I love raising Maddy in the city, the electric opportunity of it, and her schools have offered her much that suburban Bagby did not offer me academically and socially, and real-worldly (field trips to France and Nicaragua, among others; a common field trip for my classes took us to the local Wonder Bread factory). I regret, however, that Maddy has not had the freedom to run about, aimlessly and/or purposefully, on a field as big and open as Bagby's. This field is big enough to hold six full-size football or soccer games at once. It is bounded on two sides by boxed-in playgrounds, and in one corner a baseball backstop, but it is mostly open terrain.

When you approach Bagby, it's the field you see first, the school sitting along the back edge of the lot, a seeming afterthought. Play is what comes first, the field says, and play is what we lived for. No, more serious than play. For teachers and parents, I'm sure, recess is a welcome necessity, a burning off of excess energy by their charges that makes the following hours less addled for everyone. After lunch, or at the morning or afternoon recess bells, we were set free in the field to . . . *gambol* seems the most appropriate verb.

Our name for this expanse was most appropriate: we just called it "the field." The field was not a finely manicured croquet pitch; it was much wilder. The grass was mowed every so often—I used to be able to smell the freshly cut mounds of clippings from blocks away—but it was never manicured. The grass on the field, then and today, is consistently long and unruly, six to ten inches high in places, its blades thick and scratchy.

While the field may appear level, it's far from it. In the center, there's a depression in the same spot as when I used to play there, a low, almost swamp-like oval that stays muddy from November through June, several months after the last rains; near the upper-grade playground is the highest peak in the field, a dirt-packed hillock. Gopher holes abound throughout, as well as unaccountable dips and rises, all of which twist ankles. And because the earth below the grass is so well covered, it provides an endless supply of dirt clods, essential to the arsenals of many battles.

Wildlife is plentiful in the field: caterpillars, spiders, pill bugs, grasshoppers, blue-bellied lizards, garter snakes, frogs and toads, swallows and seagulls, moles and squirrels. In April of fifth grade, I unearthed a rotting log, where I found a colony of ladybugs, an undulating puddle of red and black. I didn't question it then, but now, I cannot for the life of me figure out how that log got there, a hundred yards from any tree, nor how that colony of ladybugs remained unmolested until I stumbled on it. That's how big the field was.

The field was a rough-and-tumble world, and I often judged the worth of my day at school by how much of the field I brought home with me—dirt stains on my elbows, grass stains on my jeans, the size of the new holes in those jeans, the little flecks of gravel, grass, and dirt embedded in my flesh, maybe a fresh scab or two.

The field also served as a social training ground, where one might be happy to be alone among others, huddled in groups of two or three, or joined up with bigger herds. I might play football in that corner with John Egan and Drew Burgess and Augie Amato; trade Matchbox cars by the backstop with Neal Robb and Tim Larkin; finalize a *Time Machine* and *Green Hornet* sleepover with Tracy Wilson; or run around with those girls over there, Suzanne Gallagher, Julie Basolo, and Vicky Olah, who seem to be playing keep-away or tag. Or I might request a private audience with Amy Burgraff, exiled on this vast plain, in which I would finally tell her how I felt about her—I *like-liked* her. I did make that confession, by the way, and it did not go well, but I was offered solace by the size of the field, which was as desolate a moor as any Brontë ever strode. Solitude, too, can be educational, one more aspect of the social experience.

Bordering the field were playgrounds that offered more structured, though equally invigorating activities. Between the classrooms and the grass, on a narrow

stretch of blacktop, tetherball poles rang out, and hopscotch and four-square arenas were traced in white
paint. These game areas were never empty at recess;
entire leagues and systems of etiquette were involved in
managing them. There were always one or two teachers with us at recess, who, armed with tinny whistles,
attempted to keep order, but the real rules of the playground were set and established by students and students alone, an education in social contracts. At Maddy's
lower school, the fifth-grade girls sat on top of the monkey bars, only sitting and not monkeying around a bit.
One was not allowed to sit here until one arrived in
fifth grade, and trespassing was a serious violation. No
games, these.

Along the edge of Bagby's blacktop were two boxed-in
play yards, one for first through third grades, the other
for fourth through sixth, a separation designed to cur-
tail elementary school's most pervasive tyranny, big
kids over little kids. These playgrounds were defined
by wooden planks that contained the safety material of
that era: tanbark. The tanbark at Bagby was redwood
bark, a soft, almost hairy substance that traveled well
when thrown but didn't land hard; it came in chunks
that could be five inches long and nearly two inches
wide. As we played on it, it dissolved, but was eventually replaced with a fresh supply, usually over the
summer, a back-to-school cause for celebration. While
we thought tanbark was for throwing, it was actually
intended to cushion us when we fell from the metal
play structures we climbed like the nimble critters that

we were—that's why they call these structures jungle gyms and monkey bars.

Today most of the old playground equipment has been replaced by ostensibly safer equipment. Unlike other contemporary playgrounds, however, Bagby still uses tanbark, instead of the more common recycled rubber found everywhere else. This tanbark makes me happy—in a rather inane way; nostalgia will do that— but I also see that the tanbark of today is not of the same quality as its earlier cousin. Clearly no longer redwood, it's blond, and the pieces are smaller and do not throw well at all. You kids, you just don't know . . .

To be honest, though, most contemporary playground equipment is of a more exciting order than fifty years ago. The most common "big" piece of equipment in San Francisco playgrounds looks something like the mast of a sailing ship, from which grids of rope extend to the base, which is round and turns. You climb thirty feet into the air on these ropes, while your pals spin the base of the structure, and you fly in circles. Nostalgia's all well and good, but this new play structure is not something I could even have imagined as a child.

Shockingly—and quite dangerously, I would think— there's one play structure at Bagby left over from my time there, and it happens to have been my favorite. It's a climbing structure of steel poles and hoops, about six feet high. But the design is what's key: a rocket ship. This structure reflected not only the designs and values of the community but also its highest aspirations. And those aspirations are writ large on Bagby's walls, too.

When I was in fourth grade, the school's students designed and created a mosaic, about ten feet by ten feet, that's still affixed to one end of a classroom wing. Its nine panels, each formed from colored pieces of broken tile, represent what we imagined life was and could be. There's a garden of flowers, the school itself with attendant flagpole, a profile of Abraham Lincoln, a kitten, a puppy. There is one theme, however, that repeats in four variations: space travel—a rocket about to launch; the moon and the stars; an astronaut afloat; splashdown. The mosaic reminds me of who we wanted to be and where we wanted to go; of what ambitions this ambitious, and yet average, school wanted to deliver to us.

Today I stop to consider how far I traveled in the seven years I spent at Bagby. I was, as I said earlier, fortunate to be an average student—supported at home by my parents and at school by my teachers. I enjoyed school most days, but hated it on others; I got mostly Bs, whatever that meant to me back then, but did not feel waylaid by a C now and then. And despite my averageness, or maybe even because of it, school, the fairly average school I attended, did its work. When I entered kindergarten I could barely tie my shoes, but when I left sixth grade, average though I was, I harbored the dream of becoming an astrophysicist who might one day decode the spectra of distant stars. School had pushed me beyond who I had thought I was and into the future.

II

Matriculation

II

Medication

In Between

Poor junior high school. Or middle school, or intermediate school. Whatever you call it, it is a place that's
all in between, an island of misfits. Middle schoolers
are between the ages of eleven and fifteen, typically
grades six through eight these days, certainly no longer children though a far stretch from being reasonable adults. Of the many metamorphoses I underwent
in junior high, my shift in musical tastes offers the
widest poles; I entered seventh grade singing Bobby
Goldsboro's sappy ballad "Honey" but left listening
to the dark strains of the Beatles' "Helter Skelter." In
Maddy's middle school classrooms, you'll find boys who
are barely five feet tall next to fleshed-out Amazonian
girls. Some of her fellow students go to school in
sweatpants, as if still in their pajamas, while others
arrive elaborately costumed in the full regalia of the
high school students they'll soon be. Some still trade
Pokémon cards or Peek-a-Poohs at recess, while others
wouldn't be caught dead without their makeup or flat

hats or iPods or cell phones, and on occasion, a learner's permit and the keys to the family car.

In most other countries, students tend to go straight from lower to upper school, but in the United States it's as if we've decided that puberty is such a strange and dark time, the onset of hormones and thoughts of sex so awkward and consuming, that we might as well strand these changelings on their own islands and turn away our gaze while they undergo their painful metamorphoses.

After visiting Bagby, and traveling memory's corridors from kindergarten to sixth grade, I felt compelled to visit my junior high school, to follow the matriculation from the pleasantly bucolic world of my childhood to the darker realms of adolescence. For me, as I suspect for the rest of us, more than mere subject matter changes in the summer of our twelfth years.

Oddly, though, I did not make an appointment to visit Ida Price Intermediate School. Obeying a rash and appropriately adolescent impulse, disregarding authority and its regulations, I snuck onto the school's campus on a Friday afternoon, its classes and clubs done for the week and the school practically deserted. I was trespassing, which in many ways is what the middle school years are all about, crossing boundaries that were previously inviolable. There was a cleaning crew on campus when I arrived and one of the main gates was unlocked, so I simply stepped into my own past again, a memory thief.

From the school's cafetorium steps, which overlook a large, grassy quad, I was struck not by how much time

I had spent at Ida Price, as I had at Bagby, but how much I had changed, literally transformed, in the very short time I spent here, grades seven and eight. When I began seventh, I was a football-playing wannabe astronaut; I sported a military buzz cut, black plastic glasses, and "dickies" under my straight-kid camp shirts. When I left Ida Price two years later, I was half a foot taller and determined to become a rock star; my hair flowed past my shoulders, I wore hippie wire-frame glasses and bell bottoms decorated with peace sign and Zig-Zag patches. When I entered Price, I thought girls were cute and smelled good; when I left, my thoughts of girls were of a more urgent and beguiling order.

No, that's only the surface; the changes in my life went deeper than this, and were more broadly resonant with the wider world. The space race of my elementary school years had culminated in the *Apollo* moon landing on July 20, 1969, the summer before I began seventh grade, and the news reports in our home had shifted to more complicated issues, the war in Vietnam first and most pressing among them. My brother, by then a marine staff sergeant, was continually volunteering for duty in Vietnam, "to save the world from Communism," while my father, a career navy man, who had originally supported the war, was gradually changing his mind. In seventh grade, prompted by readings from the school's librarian and in my civics class, I began to oppose the war rather stridently; the arguments in our home were fierce and loud.

Then, in May of seventh grade, on the night of the

Kent State shootings, my father died of a heart attack. During my first year of junior high, my father and I remained close, though as puberty latched on to me more tensions arose between us—we argued about my long hair and his smoking. Still, we spent a good deal of time together, exploring the world, which my father knew any education must include, and he continued to support me in my school work, especially in math and science, a knowledge his navy career had given him. As an eighth-grade dropout during the Depression, a fact of which he was somewhat ashamed, my father was determined I would succeed; graduating from high school was an achievement he considered significant and mandatory.

The death of a parent, at any time, drives a brutal and disorienting wedge into one's life, a stark boundary between the Eden before it and the chaos after. My father's death opened up for me a bottomless absence that has never completely filled.

That I was twelve years old at the time, and assaulted by all the other changes in my body and my world, meant that my father's death shaped me in ways I would not understand for many years. It seems to me now that his death had two natural but contradictory effects. First, there was the loss of order, the sense that the world could turn chaotic in an instant, and that without my father's presence, chaos ruled the days. Such essential order swept from my life, I began to do stupid, dangerous, lawless things—what was the point in following the rules if the rules were so capricious?

Coupled with this formless grief, my father's death also made me feel as if I were suddenly a fully empowered adult, ejected from the safety of childhood and in charge of a vessel under my own command. I had no idea what I was doing, but was certain I knew why I was doing it, a volatile combination. By the end of my eighth-grade year I'd been summoned to the principal's office, where I was accused of trying to buy barbiturates from a friend's older brother; that accusation was true but it only hinted at the full extent of the danger I was in.

If there's one word that describes junior high for me, it's *confusion*. Once an average student, I became an undeniably poor one, and outside school, I was on a collision course with big-time trouble.

But the confusion of those years, while not dispelled by my school and its teachers, was considerably mitigated by them, as, one teacher at a time, they made my troubled waters more navigable. In the end, school would, in a profound but simple way, save me.

The U.S. institution of junior high school is even more recent than kindergarten. Senior high school first appeared in this country in Boston and Philadelphia in the 1820s, and by the 1880s, its form was established: a wider curriculum, a broader population base, a pedagogy suited to adolescents. But it wasn't until 1909, in Columbus, Ohio, and Berkeley, California, that junior high first appeared. By the end of the 1920s, however, junior high schools had been established nationwide.

One innovation that led to this new kind of campus

was the school bus. Given that the population was still quite rural—in 1913, 50 percent of all American students attended one-room schoolhouses—the school bus made it possible for students to travel farther and attend larger schools. This shift was also abetted when more school districts began to require older students to continue beyond elementary school. Even the least academically inclined members of the population were given the opportunity—albeit by law—to receive further education. And because more American students were now enrolled in lower grades, one-room schoolhouses and local elementary schools were suddenly overcrowded.

Over the nineteenth century, teaching methods had become more effective and efficient. Teaching colleges, or "normal" schools, as they were once called, sprang up around the nation, and educational theorists and experimenters—Horace Mann, then later John Dewey, along with a host of others—made teaching more of a science and an art than it had ever been. Students studied an expanded repertoire of subjects, including the more "vocational" ones, and they were learning each subject with greater proficiency. There was also a keener awareness of the intellectual and emotional development of young teenagers. Junior high school students were not ready for the high school curriculum, but they were ready to leave elementary school.

Grammar, or elementary, school wants to provide the basic skills and sets of facts a student needs to proceed. Rhetoric, or secondary, school wants to put those skills and facts into motion. Junior high school is where we learn to change grammar into rhetoric; where science becomes experiment, scales become music, reading becomes writing rather than penmanship, facts produce action, knowledge is given force. Junior high school is a bridge from the classroom to the world.

Ida Price was built in the same decade as my elementary school, and it was certainly designed in the same spirit, if not by the same architects. It's a California suburban campus: wings of stucco classrooms, eave-shrouded halls, exterior doorways, vast playing fields. Only more of everything. Though Price may seem a supersized version of my elementary school, there are simple but crucial differences that point to school's continual desire to expand the student's involvement in the world—to *match and extend* the student's desire to become more involved.

By far the most important change in the school's structure was the student's relationship to the classroom. We no longer had one classroom but several. Each morning, twenty or so of us met in a "homeroom," where one teacher quickly prepared us for the coming day: Pledge of Allegiance, school announcements, a brief radio broadcast over the PA system, the general attempt to focus and quiet our exuberances. After homeroom, we bounced all around the campus, moving from classroom to classroom, subject to subject, and crucially, teacher to teacher. Gone was the one room, the one desk, the one teacher, that sense of insular security.

And each classroom demanded a sharper, more quickly attained focus. The classroom was not a place in which we studied *everything;* it was a place where we gathered to follow one subject much more deeply. My seventh-grade schedule: homeroom, math, civics, English, P.E., music, science, French, and either woodshop or art (one semester of each).

Because the classroom was used for only one subject, it could reflect and amplify that subject. In civics, Mr. Brock had roll upon roll of pull-down maps, a great interchangeable series of them, from the entire world to specific Civil War battles. In Mr. Williams's woodshop, there were workbenches, table and band saws, vises, planes and chisels, rows of tools any craftsperson would envy. In the girls' counterpart, home economics—such were the times—a fully stocked professional kitchen was complemented by enough sewing machines to start a sweatshop. In art, surrounded by easels and paints and pottery wheels, I never lacked for a new piece of drawing paper. This is another quite telling example of the luxury of school, access to all these tools, and through them, the ideas they promote.

Maddy's eighth-grade science room is a fully equipped laboratory: high tables with Bunsen burners, sinks, microscopes for everyone, cages with reptiles and small mammals, stores of chemicals and minerals, flats of frogs in formaldehyde, a plastic human torso that reveals its inner workings, robotics kits, posters of the periodic table and Hubble's infinite galaxies and the freshwater fish of Bangladesh. When we toured possible middle schools for

Maddy, we found some with classrooms that were all but bare, the worst of chalk and talk, drill and kill. When we first saw the SF Friends School classrooms, each stuffed with "educational" materials, I knew it was a school that would offer Maddy a more engaged, rather than passive, academic life. All the tools a student needed, as well as the time and focus to master them. I could imagine what she'd do with those tools, how she might progress from textbook to scalpel.

Ida Price offered me the tools I had been prepared since kindergarten to put to use. It is a source of great dismay and anger to me that art and crafts and music too, along with the more applied sciences, are no longer offered in such abundance, if at all, in today's California public schools (Maddy's middle school is private, hence the superbly supplied classes). What I once took for granted is now something viewed as *extra, superfluous;* the luxury has been diminished. See: Bake Sale.

Ideally, when free to move around this changed and much larger campus, middle school students find ever new methods of ownership. Because of the size of the campus, there were more students at Price, and they came from a wider geographical range; we met and mingled with kids from beyond our own neighborhoods, discovering that there were others out there, new kids strangely familiar but yet unknown. Junior high should be a more social time in one's life, and the size of the student body ensured new friendships and rivalries, and so we gathered.

Unlike Bagby, but with some clear intention, the classrooms at Price did not open directly onto the playing fields but rather onto four separate *quads,* open plazas littered with stone benches. Though officially an "intermediate school," we called Price a junior high, fittingly and with some bravado. We were on our way to high school, the school's design told us, and so we reached for what lay ahead.

At Price, some students still fled to the playing fields at recess or lunch, but others of us, those who were ready to move on to new social contracts, gathered in the open quads, boys and girls together, perhaps for the first time, talking and talking, pairing up and breaking up. Only the year before Jeff Smith, Keith Epstein, Neal Robb, Jim Bryant, and I were content to play sports at every recess and primarily with other boys, but now we spent our recess time in the quad talking with Cindy Roberts, Cheri Miller, Candee Hooper, Terry Stahl, Cindy Blackmon, Michelle Sanz, and Chris MacAdams. Photos from my yearbooks confirm this. What were we talking about? No matter, we were talking. We sat together in new formations, trying on the masks of romance and novel forms of friendship. We might have been playacting at this more adult activity, but this was no child's play. Offered the chance to do so by the school's architecture, we gathered on benches in the bright California sun, to socialize and become socialized.

As important as the quads in our blossoming social lives were our lockers. I remember the allure, when leaving sixth grade, of the junior high locker, an object that seemed dazzling, dangerous almost, as if it might explode if handled incorrectly. What had appealed to me, of course, was that my locker locked, and for adolescents, secrecy is a key ingredient to a satisfying life. The novelist John Irving claims that adolescence is when we begin to keep secrets from those we most love; he gets that right. More so than my elementary school desk, my locker was my castle, and only I had the keys to it (well, the combination).

Price's open-air halls were lined with pods of lockers, narrow metal closets with plenty of interior surface for decorating—oh, you could put your books there, too, and some stinky athletic clothes. These might seem only displaced versions of the elementary school desk, a repository for school supplies, emblematic posters, cryptic talismans, contraband. But your locker was also a social station, where you met with your friends, where you knew to find someone, or where you knew to look, from afar, for someone between classes, even if you weren't going to actually talk to Sue Anderson.

My years-long friendship with Rich Davis began because our lockers, by random assignment, were next to each other. Meeting Rich, though accidental, signaled another big shift in my life. Jim Bryant had been my *best-best* friend since second grade, and while there was no rift between us, we were beginning to drift apart; Jim would take a more studious route, a more sober path, while I, especially after my father's death, had climbed on something of a roller coaster. Rich Davis would be my perfect companion for that ride. Rich, who had gone to Steindorf Elementary, was skinny as a rail, my first *long-haired* friend, and he played the drums. He was also a major league wiseass and back talker, which I found irresistible and which liberated my own inner wiseass. The youngest of five, Rich, for whatever family dynamics were at work in that crowded house, was also entering a reckless phase. By the time I finished junior high, I dressed more like Rich than Jim Bryant, and wore my hair accordingly, played my new bass guitar in Rich's band, and together, Rich and I pursued new and ever more lawless excitements. Jim Bryant remained a good friend, but Rich was now my closest companion, for good *and* for ill, and though we would go to different high schools, thanks to district border changes, we remained inseparable until I went off to college. All this thanks to a locker assignment.

Oddly enough, given our new freedoms, some of us began to spend more time at school rather than racing home. We *volunteered* to stay after school for extracurricular activities. The school's more intense and focused curriculum aided this—we began to discover our little passions. At Ida Price there were intercollegiate and intramural sports, of course, but also Chess Club, A/V Club, French Club, Ecology Club, various choruses and orchestras, and more. Maddy's schools have offered her a mind-boggling assortment of extracurricular activity: painting, sculpting, yoga, Mandarin, tae kwon do, violin or piano or xylophone or rock band, ballet and tap and modern and Afro-Cuban dance, filmmaking, even a class in Legos.

The extracurricular activity that most occupied my seventh- and eighth-grade years was Drama Club. The cafetorium at Ida Price was of the same design as my elementary school's—hot-lunch line and tables that folded into the walls. Price's stage, however, was not a shallow, curtained platform, but rather a true theater with a deep backstage, and a full bank of stage sets and lights. I discovered in seventh grade that I had become something of a ham—a trait fostered if not created by my new and more "adult" social skills—and I was thrilled to discover that I might find an audience for my new extroversion. But performances were the least of Drama Club, I soon found out. Each fall and spring we spent our afternoons preparing two full-length plays, auditioning, building sets, sewing costumes, rehearsing our lines and blocking our movements, only eventually taking our brief bows. During these long, luxurious hours, we made something bigger than the sum of its parts. All through high school, I continued in Drama Club, not so much with dreams of Broadway as for that invigorating camaraderie—a lot of work, a whole bunch of fun, and some valuable lessons snuck in as well.

The plays we put on at Price were not the classics of world theater but trite melodramas, whose broad emotions seemed appropriate only for junior high. In one yearbook photo, Jeff Smith, the funniest kid in school, is decked out in cape, top hat, and villainous mustache, and he is threatening my leading lady, Jeri Harkleroad, whom I was obliged to kiss after I had saved her from peril. Jeri and I did not kiss during rehearsals, saving it for the performances, but we did kiss then. School was preparing us for many things.

Price's cafetorium was also the site of school dances, an innovation I didn't know my life was lacking until it appeared suddenly. We came to school at night, not for our recitals or teacher conferences, but for an evening that belonged solely to us, an occasion for working out some of our more pressing social complications.

In San Jose, in 1970, a school dance required a live band made up of shaggy teenage boys and their guitars and amplifiers. Maddy's dances, at school and in other community venues, use no live bands, only DJs. The music at Maddy's dances might be a little better for the DJs, but something is missing, if only the chance for groups of shaggy teenage boys (and more girls now, happily) to trot out their garage-created songs and bad radio-hit covers.

The cafetorium on dance night was transformed into a cavernous nightclub by the addition of crepe paper streamers and balloons. But these decorations were hardly visible, as if they were present only to highlight the much-desired darkness. The adults in attendance were mere chaperones, enough of them to contain the madness of junior high, but not nearly enough to prevent the sneakier troubles we might get into. There was, I recall clearly, a "ruler rule"; couples were to be twelve inches apart while dancing, and chaperones attempted to reinforce that gap with actual rulers. To no avail. My memories of these nights are of the swaying gropes we called "slow" dances. Pam Chase was the first girl I slow-danced with, to a very long version of Donovan's "Atlantis"; it was not a romantic song at all, but I didn't object. Dark enough and space enough.

After my first seventh-grade dance, I waited at the curb for my parents to pick me up. It was dark, I was out alone in the night, the school was mine, and I had danced with girls. Drunk on sugary sodas, my ears ringing from loud music, I knew, viscerally, that everything in my life was changing, both inside and out.

While I was undergoing puberty, and all its confusions, and being brought into closer contact, socially and physically, with girls, those beings who were causing me so much of the confusion, my school and its changing structures seemed, somewhat cruelly, to want to highlight these improbable changes, to point out our physical metamorphoses rather than hide them. I'm speaking, of course, about P.E.

Physical education has long been an integral part of school life. Many historians of education believe that some of the first formal schools in the West were military in nature, as at Sparta, because such specialized training required a centralized and cohesive structure,

as opposed to the vocational training that happened at
home and in the fields. Military training mandated rigorous physical conditioning.

At Bagby, recess was the only school activity that
came close to exercise, and that seemed enough to me,
but in junior high, all that changed; P.E. was a graded
part of the curriculum. No longer were we set free on
big lawns to organize our own games; instead, we played
team sports under coaches' supervision, wore gym
clothes, performed "calisthenics." While I had played
league and sandlot baseball in lower school, and both
my father and brother were adept at athletics—boxing
and football, respectively—in junior high, rock and roll
held eminence over any sport for me. Sports seemed, to
my Beatle-flushed brain, to be quite uncool.

But there was another reason I did not like P.E. Sur-
prisingly, and horrifyingly, we had to get naked for it.
Naked in front of one another. Naked and cold and shiv-
ering in the locker room, a vast bunker-like structure
wisely placed a hundred yards from our classrooms. We
undressed, dressed, sweated, undressed, showered, re-
dressed, all in plain view of our peers. I had been a fat
kid most of my life, and even though early puberty had
stretched me out, when I stepped into the locker room,
I still held that old image of myself. The locker room
can still be, for some of us adults, a vulnerable occasion,
but for middle schoolers, one must count it as torture.
It's reasonable that our coaches made us shower—
adolescents can be mighty rank—but in middle school,
your body is doing all sorts of crazy things, and exposing

these transformations, or *lack* of them, can make a P.E. shower the longest five minutes of the day.

The playing fields at Price had grown and evolved to meet our more organized sports needs. The campus boasted several basketball courts, one inside the cafetorium, but the others were plein air: a crushed-granite running track with attendant hurdles, and long- and high-jump pits; a baseball backstop, complete with dugouts, bleachers, and a snack bar; a handful of football fields and soccer pitches. In high school, add two pools, one for racing and one for diving; two gyms, one for basketball, volleyball, and Deathball, and one for gymnastics, with trampolines and pommel horses and parallel and uneven bars; tennis courts; a lighted football stadium and track. We were the children of President John F. Kennedy's physical education initiatives, and we had federally mandated fitness tests four times a year.

Today, in California at least, P.E. is no longer required in nearly the same number of hours: blame budget cuts again. These cuts to the P.E. curriculum do nothing to abate the childhood obesity epidemic and those now much larger desks. I never warmed to P.E. and spent a considerable amount of energy trying to get out of it, but I do wish we still had more of it. Not all of us will become spandex-clad weekend warriors as adults, but to be made to go outside and run laps can be as energizing for the mind as for the body.

For me, the most positive change in junior high was my relationship to my teachers. Junior high, when we sail off into the murky waters of puberty, is a difficult enough time as it is. And certainly the expanded social life middle school offers is distracting. Seeing school merely as a place to meet up with one's peers and devise new capers, many students during these years struggle to get the same grades they'd earned in elementary school. But my father's death precipitated an academic slide that lasted for several years. I was no longer an average student gradewise, but decidedly below average, bringing home Cs and Ds.

In the intervening years, I often looked back on that time and thought my junior high teachers saved me *after* the storm of my father's death swamped me. But looking more closely today, I see that my chronology is somewhat skewed. The help I received from my teachers back then started early in seventh grade, *before* my father's death, so that when the real trouble blew over the horizon, the relationships with my teachers, which would keep me from drowning completely, were already in place. And it was the design of junior high itself that made these important connections possible.

I remember my elementary school teachers with a great fondness—there was comfort and security and inspiration there. Each of my teachers, from kindergarten through sixth grade, were important figures in my life and, I can see clearly now, still are. But because those were my only teachers during a year, and they had twenty students every day for the entire year, my relationship with them was most often at a comfortable distance. There was simply not the time for these teachers to instruct us one-on-one for more than a few necessary moments. They remained, most often, at the head of the classroom.

I recall my junior high teachers more distinctly as individuals, even though I spent less time with them. Because I had a wider range of teachers in junior high—up to ten a year—it was more likely I'd find one or two who really understood me and were willing to push our lessons beyond the textbook and the classroom.

This was still junior high, however, and many of the teachers at Ida Price were subject to our scorching derision, which we saw as a signal of our "sophistication," but which was probably more about forging, rather recklessly, sharper senses of ourselves (or maybe we were just annoying middle school students). Mr. Crappuchette, our music teacher, was a mousy little man, nattily dressed, whose name is one of the more unfortunate teacher names ever recorded; he didn't stand a chance. Mrs. Dimbleby, math, was at once so timid and so filled with a boiling frustration, that I shudder to recall her explosions. Mrs. Lamy, French, was a blowsy, flamboyant woman who dressed younger than she ought to have, and due to her flamboyance, was fair game for our less-than-pointed wit. We were often merciless to these and to many other teachers, and I never thought of them then as teachers I "liked."

But it's interesting to note that good teachers, at least those who prove effective in the long run, need not be the most popular teachers, the "cool" teachers. Mr. Crappuchette's lessons on the bass and treble clefs have remained with me. Mrs. Dimbleby did go out of her way at a parent-teacher conference to offer me help

with algebra. Mrs. Lamy made French both compre-
hensible and enjoyable enough that I would continue to
study it through high school and college, eventually
speaking it on the streets of Paris. Their lessons, reluc-
tantly received, stuck.

I have a good friend who speaks of her school years
with nothing but scorn—she is not alone in this—
except when speaking of the teacher in charge of her
marching band. He is, she tells me, someone she still
thinks about, whose influence she considers important. I once asked her if she and this teacher had one of
those movie relationships in which they had long, deep
conversations, where she'd finally found an adult she
could confide in. No, she told me; she had rarely spoken to him one-on-one, and most of what she gleaned
from him came while she stood with her clarinet in the
middle of a football field under a scorching sun. His influence on her had been one of quiet example.

I am happy, today at least, to have had these effective
if "uncool" teachers. But for me, the best of my junior
high experience centered on the deeper relationship
between student and mentor, and the surprising ways
these mentors found and fostered me.

Not all our teachers are found at school. By junior high,
if not well before, many students begin to study under
coaches and instructors outside school. But teachers,
nonetheless.

In seventh grade, at Rich Davis's urging (if I learned
to play an instrument, he told me, I could join his band),

I signed up for bass guitar lessons (the instrument the band needed most). Once a week for four years, I balanced my cheap knockoff of Paul McCartney's violin-shaped Hofner on the handlebars of my bike and headed out to Guitar Showcase, a remodeled ranch house–cum–music shop, where John Sharkey taught me to make orderly noise with this simple instrument. Like all good teachers, though, Sharkey taught me more than the subject at hand; he taught me about myself.

How easy it was to fall under his thrall. Sharkey was cool, no doubt about it, a short, ropy guy who dressed in the standard rock 'n' roll garb of the day: frayed bell bottoms, irreverent T-shirts, shaded glasses, really long hair. A former member of the Syndicate of Sound, a local band that had shone nationally for fifteen minutes—"Little Girl" was their big hit—he was a wizard guitarist with an insatiable hunger for all music. But he was a demanding teacher, and because of that, I loved entering his classroom, an erstwhile bedroom the size of a closet, where we worked together.

My desire, of course, was to become—overnight if possible—a great guitarist, but much to my chagrin, Sharkey taught me to play scales first and foremost, convinced me that one didn't master an instrument, or even play it well, without endless hours devoted to the basics. If I didn't learn this simple lesson, he told me, there was no hope. He taught me, too, that being a bass player was about "laying down the law," and not showing off; no one, he was correct in pointing out, ever wanted to listen to a bass solo.

Most importantly, perhaps, he filled my ears with new music, music I was unfamiliar with and often didn't like at first—Delta blues, rockabilly, bebop and cool jazz, polished pop, rhythm and blues, country, classical. He'd say, "Go buy this," play me a track or two on a portable turntable, and I'd somehow scrounge together the $2.99 an LP cost. He taught me to listen so that I might be able to play. Sharkey made me love music even more than I already did, and he made me love it by teaching me what I did not know. This is the first lesson: what you do not know.

One afternoon, early in my years of lessons, the power at Showcase went out, the practice rooms and amps all dark. I was ready to call it a day, but Sharkey refused to let the opportunity pass, so we cleared a space in the front display windows, where there was just enough light, and we played acoustically. This was yet another key piece of educational wisdom: keep your lessons, no matter what, no matter how you are feeling or what else might be calling you. It's important to be present. If you don't show up, nothing will happen. This lesson is one that every good teacher and mentor I've had since has reemphasized.

It was a good thing we held that blacked-out lesson. That gray winter afternoon in the front window, Sharkey tried to teach me a funk riff far more complicated than the slow blues I was still trying to get down. He played the riff at full speed, then slowly, in pieces, which was his habit. I watched and tried to copy him, but I kept muffing it.

"I can't do it," I finally said. "I just can't."

"Yes you can," he said.

He played again; I muffed it again.

"I can't," I said.

"No," he said. "You can. You just won't."

"What?"

"You *can* do it," he said. "You're *capable* of doing it. You *can;* you just *won't.* You're giving up. You can; you just won't."

And he shrugged then, ready to give up on me if I was willing to give up on myself.

That was a life-changing moment, understanding the difference between capacity and willingness. Over the years, in so many different arenas—playing music, writing, school work, and personal and professional struggles—that simple phrase of Sharkey's has often returned to me. In that one phrase, I received a glimpse of a deep and abiding truth. I *could* play that riff, of course, but *would* I? Would I push myself to make it happen? I did eventually get that riff, not then but later that night practicing in my room. I did it by trying again and again, by force of will.

Today, I still play bass a few times a year with some old friends, though I have long forgotten most of the riffs Sharkey taught me. I have never forgotten his most important lessons, however, which had nothing to do with the bass guitar. Sharkey taught me to teach myself.

I graduated from Ida Price in 1971, a heady time for "current events" in the United States, the country in turmoil, the war ever present, as if it all might come bursting through our front door at any minute. My eighth-grade civics teacher was Mrs. Tullis, and each week our class waded through current events, poring over newspapers and magazines she brought in for us and that we also brought from home. If we were going to learn about civics, she told us, we had to be citizens, too, engaged participants. There was no dividing line between our textbooks and the world, she wanted us to understand.

Though my navy father was now dead, my Marine Corps brother, recently mustered out, was still quite hawkish, and debates about the war still filled my head and our living room. I was, as most of my generation's teenagers were, adamantly opposed to the war, but I was ignorant of the war's history and the larger picture, and confused, perhaps most of all, by the role regular soldiers played in Vietnam's carnage—my brother and cousins and their friends, who were ordered to kill and be killed.

So in the fall of eighth grade, I turned—without much forethought—to Mrs. Tullis. She was not, as might be expected, the "hippie" teacher in peasant blouse and beads, but rather "establishment" looking. Her hair was helmet-sprayed in an audacious flip, and she wore dresses any "straight" woman would have worn then, various polyesters in styles that predated Woodstock. But she was passionate about current events, and wanted to help us make up our own minds about what we read; she insisted that we learn to read the world "through" the media instead of merely accepting the world the media presented to us.

One day I stopped by Mrs. Tullis's classroom during her free period, with a question about the Free Speech movement in Berkeley. I knew that the Free Speech movement and the protests against the war in Vietnam were tethered somehow, but I didn't understand the connection. It was a hot, bright Indian summer afternoon, and we stayed in her classroom the entire period, wading through stacks of magazines and newspapers. When school let out that day, I returned to her room, at her invitation, and we continued our research.

It would have been easy—and more than reasonable— for Mrs. Tullis to beg off this project, to point me to one article, or to offer a five-minute capsule version, or simply claim she had too much on her already crowded plate. But Mrs. Tullis knew of my father's death and the subsequent slide of my grades, and had often held out a steadying hand. That day in her classroom, she guided me through the thorny mess of Vietnam and the Free Speech movement, article by article, first showing me the connections that were necessary, then asking me to make my own connections. With her guidance, but under my own steam, I came to draw a deeper, though still messy, portrait of the world I was becoming more aware of each day.

Mrs. Tullis continued to open her door to me that year, and together we delved deeper and deeper into larger and larger landscapes.

She could easily have said no.

My understanding of the war in Vietnam began in Mrs. Tullis's classroom and continued to occupy me for years to come. But as with my guitar lessons, what prevails today is not the actual "content" but something more precious. She and I became, I liked to believe then, friends, though that friendship, that intimacy, was a disguise for a more important relationship; no longer just my teacher, she was now my mentor. Here was an adult—a stranger, really—who took the time to take me seriously, who showed me I could, and should, move beyond myself into what I did not yet know. She was not concerned with what she taught me, the content, but with the simple idea that I could learn to think for myself. She never once insisted on her own opinion in any of my studies, but elicited mine instead. Not *what* she taught but *how;* not *what* I learned but *how.*

Mrs. Tullis was exactly who I needed at that moment. I was stepping into an ever more confusing world, but there was a mentor beside me now, a guide, who, ill paid for her efforts, freely offered her space and time.

Mrs. Tullis was far from the last of my mentors. High school was ahead of me, and the confusions that began after my father's death only deepened and became more dangerous, accompanied, of course, by entirely new confusions. Junior high school and its broadening horizons, its offer of closer relationships with more teachers, had done much to help keep me righted after my father's death. But in high school, I discovered a raft of other and even more crucial mentors. I would discover that I was not alone on the voyage.

Open Campus

After wading through the junior high years, it seemed impossible to put a stop to my memory tour; the tug had become too strong. I was no longer examining school in its broadest landscapes but following a more intimate thread, that of my own life and how school had rescued me. Either feeling guilty over my junior high trespass of a few weeks previous, or tapping into the more mature self that had graduated from high school, this time I arranged an official tour.

When I arrived at Branham High School, on a cloud-spotted late afternoon just after classes had ended, I was not initially overcome by a strong wash of memories. Those memories would begin to appear as the tour continued, but my first thought when I stepped into the wide, locker-lined corridors was how I fit, physically, at Branham. I was an adult when I graduated in 1975, and so the scale of student to school was still correct.

Branham truly is a "senior" version of junior high, bigger in all ways than Ida Price, though in shape and substance similar. In high school, everything about junior high becomes wider and deeper, farther and further. The high school campus and its curriculum offer the student more freedoms, and commensurate opportunities and rewards. So, too, the risks are greater, because the student, aspiring to independence when offered these freedoms, might make choices, consciously or otherwise, that can permanently shape his future in troubling ways. If junior high places some students on the precipice of failure, senior high might push them off that edge. According to boostup.org, some seven thousand U.S. high school students drop out *every day* of the school year, nearly 1.3 million annually. Currently, 28 percent of U.S. seniors do not graduate, an appalling figure.

Though I had begun to flounder as a student in junior high, I was righted, if temporarily, by Mrs. Tullis and a few other teachers there. By the end of my sophomore year at Branham, however, my report cards showed a few Cs, but Ds were now the norm, and my elementary school Bs had all but disappeared. During the first two years of high school I simply did not do any homework, rarely read the assigned literature, and held on to the misplaced belief that I could fool everyone and *cool* my way through school.

Still disoriented by my father's death, freed, perilously, from his guidance and structure, and given the raft of new freedoms that high school offered, I was busy making a mess of my life. My mother, to her credit, did her best to do the impossible, that is, raise a teenage boy on her own, especially during the permissive 1970s. She set wide boundaries for me, hoping that such space would be sufficient to contain me, and I was *almost* smart enough to observe those boundaries. But I was a teenager and superbly skilled, so I believed, in making everything look all right when it wasn't.

In the summer between junior and senior high, I began to use drugs of all shapes and sizes—mescaline, LSD, uppers and downers, and of course, pot. This was 1971, and not only were drugs widely available in San Jose, but the tenor of the times recommended them—they would expand your mind, was one mantra. So I knew about drugs and was curious, and my new best friend, Rich Davis, had a raft of older siblings who were more than happy to turn us both on (Jim Bryant, much straighter than me, didn't so much sever our friendship as avoid it). All that summer Rich and I tried whatever we could get our hands on (including, I shudder to remember, Glade American Beauty Rose air freshener sprayed into a plastic bread bag). I smoked a joint on my way to the bus stop the first morning of my freshman year, a fact I counted as a kind of victory. Pot would turn out to be my drug of choice, and I was stoned pretty much every day the first two years of high school.

I began to cut school frequently, though I became more expert at forging notes and conning my mother, and I knew exactly how many absences I could rack up in a semester without getting suspended (I have never understood why students guilty of chronic truancy should get kicked *out* of school). I was rarely at home before eleven at night—either at band rehearsals with Rich and our wizard guitarist Tim Sanz, or wandering the flat suburban streets, alone or with Rich, or some combination of the stoner friends he and I drew our way. In an ironic twist, one of our favorite nighttime activities—this was San Jose; our entertainment options were limited—was to go to Bagby or another elementary school and play on the slides and swings, all while baked to a crisp.

In short, I was fucking up badly.

And it could have gotten much worse. Late in my freshman year, I was arrested for shoplifting from Macy's—the cassette version of *Woodstock II*—and despite what I told the police, it was not my first time. The arresting officer wrote "looks like a professional" in his report, and he was not wrong. I had begun to shoplift the summer before, at first beer from liquor stores, but finding that too easy, I moved on to more challenging items and was soon a dedicated thief. Together Rich and I stole six-packs of Budweiser and bottles of Cold Duck from grocery stores (we prized this cocktail not for its taste but for its efficiency), and by myself I stole LPs, cassettes, tape players, black lights, speakers, whatever I wanted actually, from stores across the Santa Clara Valley. I also stole for my friends, things they wanted but couldn't get, and which I was happy to snag for them. Rich and I even tried to steal a car once, my cousin's Jaguar, having heard that you could start a stick shift simply by pushing it (but it has to be in gear, and facing downhill; we pushed it at least a mile down the flat streets of my neighborhood before turning around and pushing it back). I was a bad kid, and stupid to boot.

Looking back on that year, along with the shame of this confession, it's horrifyingly clear today how close I was to slipping into a life I might not have escaped. Rich and I came close a couple of times to getting "set up" by dealers we knew who would front us enough pot to start our own operations. We didn't eventually, and I think the main reason is that at least we had our music, our band—thank you, John Sharkey—and to that we had remained dedicated.

Mine were not the mean streets of some failing city, mind you, but the tree-lined cul-de-sacs of a genteel, working-class suburb, and I suppose that's what is to be heeded. I was not locked into a dire fate by poverty or culture. I was a teenager who'd become unmoored, either by the loss of my father and his example, or by too much freedom, but such unmooring can happen to any student, regardless of background, family troubles, economics, what have you. Kids get lost. But kids get saved, too.

By the time I graduated from Branham, I was earning straight As, had been accepted into university, and, though still a teenager and prone to various mischiefs, found myself moving in a much more purposeful direction, and happy to be sailing that course. What changed all this? Simple: school itself.

Branham High was built in 1968, twelve years after Bagby and Ida Price, but is architecturally their sibling. The campus, though, is four times as large as Price's: the corridors are longer and the overhanging eaves wider, the playing fields impossibly vast rather than merely so, and the quads and gyms and cafetorium bigger and more varied. It's almost as if all my schools—Bagby, Price, Branham—were only one school, an organism that grew and developed along with me and my fellow students, an ever-expanding carapace.

The student body at Branham was over two thousand, enfolding four junior highs into one location. At every step of the way through school, we came to know more kids, find more houses to visit.

The single most obvious difference between Branham and my earlier schools is visible before you enter the school grounds: the parking lot. Bagby and Price had faculty parking lots, but Branham's was a student parking lot, a great asphalt steppe filled every morning and lunch period and afternoon with horsepower and chrome, raucous music, and clouds of smoke and hormones.

Branham was an "open campus," meaning we could leave at lunch to raid the 7-Eleven or Jack in the Box down the street, and on occasion, disappear for the rest of the day. In our own cars. Or our parents' cars. Three days before my sixteenth birthday, a week before my junior year began, I purchased, for three hundred busboy-earned dollars, a sparkle-green 1965 Ford Galaxie 500 the size of a fishing boat, which I drove to school every day, until, six months later, it stopped running. With some chagrin—though a willing chagrin—I then drove to school, when allowed, in my mother's powder-blue

Dodge Duster, a more compact and sedate status symbol. Still, it was a car.

As the student progresses, the geographical range
over his home territory expands, a natural progress, but
one abetted by the size and structure of his schools. At
Bagby I walked back and forth from school, but rarely
ventured out of my neighborhood on my own. In junior
high I rode my bike to Guitar Showcase and even farther, often a score of miles across the valley floor and up
into the foothills of the Santa Cruz Mountains. In the
last two years of high school, I would drive—frequently
with a carload of fellow hooky players—fifty miles or
more, radio blaring, just to be driving fifty miles or
more, up to San Francisco or down to Monterey. One
of my favorite memories of cutting class is a solitary
one. Unable to find a willing accomplice, or perhaps
not wanting one that day, I drove to Santa Cruz, on
the coast, where I spent the day on the beach greedily
and lazily reading most of *Catch-22*. An oddly studious
day for one cutting out (but I had, by that time, become
oddly studious).

At its best, school encourages the student to move
farther into the world and further into his studies. It is
one of the achievements of J. K. Rowling's Harry Potter
series that she captured this expansive movement.
When Harry, Ron, and Hermione begin their studies
at Hogwarts, their classes are basic, their movements
confined to that magical, and completely enviable, campus. As they move up through the grades, the subjects
of their classes narrow and deepen, their relationships

with their teachers grow more intimate and urgent, and they begin to roam more widely in the world, first into the adolescently apt Forbidden Forest, then the village of Hogsmeade, then into London, and finally, in their last year, completely off campus, up and down England. Granted, Harry, Ron, and Hermione are on a mission to save the world from the Dark Lord, but they are still in school.

School pushes you—lures you?—into the world. Whether, as students, we learn more widely about the world and then foray into it, or whether we dive into the world and then learn about it, is a difficult argument to parse. These are, most likely, concurrent journeys.

At Branham, the general spiral of school's focus and expansion continued to turn, both inward and outward. We followed a wider spectrum of disciplines each year, with each individual course more deeply plumbed. Instead of a year of science, we would follow a year of biology or chemistry or physics. Math broke into— much to my heavy-lidded confusion—algebra, both I and II, geometry, calculus, trigonometry (safe to say, the elegant languages of calc and trig were pleasures I avoided). English was British or American or world lit, even satire, science fiction, creative writing. Every discipline revealed deeper veins; each subject was worth, we were shown, exploring in greater detail.

I took an entire year of typing when I was a sophomore, a tedious, mechanical class, one intended, I imagined, to train the great corps of secretaries of our bureaucratic world, a class I chose because I heard it would be easy. I hated every butt-numbing hour of that class, but today, I'm grateful to be able to type seventy words a minute.

The opportunity was afforded me at Branham, should I have chosen, to learn virtually anything, to prepare myself for college or a vocation, to spin as widely and as deeply into the world as I might. Eventually, I took advantage of these opportunities. But not without a good deal of help from my teachers. As in junior high, my senior high teachers guided me both in and out of the classroom, but there was more at stake now, for me at least, more to lose and more to gain. And there was also, in this four-year structure, more time to spend with those teachers who were guiding me.

Most ex-students (though I'm not sure one is ever an ex-student) would count themselves lucky to have a single important teacher from their school days, that one teacher who helped turn things around, show them new paths, open new doors. At Branham, I was blessed with an abundance of masterful teachers, teachers learned in and passionate about their subjects, while at the same time dedicated to shaping the nonscholastic lives of their students. Branham was a new high school, with a faculty younger than most, and since this was the 1970s, the fervent and progressive idealism of the 1960s was still alive in these teachers.

In history, I had Mr. Beebe and Mr. Dragon, and one half-year substitute whose name I can't remember; they all helped me see the world as larger than I imagined, and to see myself as not unimportant but in truer scale to the world than a teenager often does. I even had an algebra teacher, Mr. Hillman, who understood that math would never be my calling; nonetheless he guided me through geometry and algebra II in extra afternoon sessions, so that I might earn the passing grades I would need to apply to California's university system. He put his passion for math second to my passion to move up and out.

Miss Long was our drama teacher, as well as the director of our student plays and musicals, and under her strict but enthusiastic guidance, we created play after play, full productions, made possible only by long hours of after-school rehearsals. She also made sure we knew the history of the American theater and read its finest works; sometimes this reading was part of a class assignment, but at other times she read with us on her own, outside school. Even then I knew how much public school teachers were paid and knew Miss Long's salary was not enough. I was—and still am—astonished by how many hours of her own life Miss Long put into our plays, how much she demanded of us, and so demanded of herself, to make those plays, well, probably just average school plays, but better than necessity and her paycheck required. She loved the theater, that was clear, and wanted us to love it, too.

In my junior year, while playing Giles Corey in Arthur Miller's *The Crucible,* I came down with a high fever and lost my voice, and tried to beg off the last two performances. Miss Long didn't insist I go on those last two nights, but she did ask me to consider the fate of the production and everyone else involved. She actually trotted out the old saw "the show must go on." I went onstage both nights, swallowing spoonfuls of glycerin between acts, and hammed it up, a rousing success, if not in the annals of American theater, at least for myself and my fellow actors. The lesson Miss Long taught me—it might have been a dangerous lesson; I was sick for weeks after—about perseverance and fortitude is one I've called on over the decades, and one that rhymes sharply with those lessons Sharkey taught me at Guitar Showcase.

In English alone, I had four years of dynamic teachers: Mr. Shibley, Mrs. Jouthas, Mrs. Weinberg, Miss Foncell. We studied Shakespeare and Twain and Faulkner and Fitzgerald, even a little Chaucer, but also Ray Bradbury, Isaac Asimov, Arthur C. Clarke, Jean Shepherd, Kurt Vonnegut, Joseph Heller, and perhaps the most influential literature of my secondary education, *Mad* magazine. The literature I studied in high school came from a well that was deep and wide. Literally, of course—and this is important to bear in mind—this literature came from Branham's well-stocked book room.

It was in my English classes that I wrote my first short stories, began to read books as if my life depended on it, and conceived a rather ambitious goal that went beyond school. All this started with a book report my sophomore year, a simple school assignment that has proved, back then and to this day, an essential turning point in my life.

Mrs. Jouthas—she of the immaculate board work—assigned a five-page report on John Steinbeck's *The Grapes of Wrath*, a book she'd chosen particularly for me. To her thoughtful recommendation I responded as only a reluctant teenager can: it was *so long*. I've seen my daughter do the same thing just this past summer, weighing a book by page count rather than possible interest. Though a failing student at the time, I did admire Mrs. Jouthas, and wanting to impress her, began—eventually and at the last possible moment—to read the novel. Late one night I read the first chapter of the book, and found myself so moved by the power of Steinbeck's words that I immediately, and without any thought beyond compulsion, wrote my first short story, convinced I had found my life's calling. That story, "The Dreamer," is a typically embarrassing piece of teenage angst, but it was the beginning of a life's dedication and reward that has continued since those first pages of purple prose.

From that night on, I became a devoted reader, too, which perhaps proved the more useful turn in my life. Writing has always been my intention, a somewhat selfish goal, but the flourishing of reading in my life introduced me, in a vivid fashion, to the larger world, and has, I hope, made me a more engaged citizen of that world. Reading certainly prepared me to move forward with my education. I might have, at some point, stepped away from writing to follow another path, but it is doubtful I would ever have dropped reading, that essential skill and pleasure. When I finished *The Grapes of Wrath,* I proceeded to read everything else Steinbeck had written, and from there moved on to Hemingway and Updike and Cheever, and an endless stream of others.

My newfound passion for reading was not merely for literature either. Once I unlocked the rewards and pleasures of reading, which had been inculcated in me ten years before in first grade, I was more than happy to read my history and psychology and science texts, that luxurious bounty school provided me. And the more I read, in all disciplines, the better I did in classes, and so I read more, and with more confidence and reward. Students like to be good at what they do, and *love* the rewards of doing it well. My new lust for reading played a large part in the renaissance of my school life. I discovered Steinbeck and reading early my sophomore year, when I was a first-class ne'er-do-well, and you can almost chart the upswing in my academic progress through my involvement in literature; by the end of that year I was starting to get my first As. All because Mrs. Jouthas put the right book in the right hands at the right time. I don't believe Mrs. Jouthas thought I would become a writer, but she suspected that I had something to learn from literature, that it could help me, and she knew me well enough as a person, not merely as a student, to know that I was ready for the challenge she offered.

I'm tempted to say of that book report that I was "struck by lightning," which credits some odd idea of

fate for my life's path, but that is a shallow and dis-
ingenuous conclusion. True enough, I had been a non-
reader for many years, but it's clear to me that school
had, in its most basic forms (reading and writing, at
least), given me the necessary tools for this "lightning"
moment. And because of all those other hours in all
those other classes, every one of my teachers urging
me to pick up my gaze and seek out the wider world,
school prepared me to be interested in the Joads and the
dust bowl of Oklahoma, then the Spanish Civil War,
the elegance and brutality of New York City, the bloody
fields of Troy and Vietnam. Whether I liked sitting in
class or not, or only half-pretended to pay attention at
school, or had days of absolute loathing for anything
vaguely related to school, that in the end was no matter.
Allow me the teacher's prerogative of repetition: one
doesn't necessarily have to enjoy the lesson for the lesson to endure.

During my difficult first two years at Branham, despite the fact that I was nearly dropping out, or perhaps
because of that fact, I was already receiving encouragement from my teachers, a support that only deepened when I found writing and reading. My English
teachers—especially Mrs. Jouthas, but all of them—
read the stories I wrote outside class, talked with me
about the books I was reading on my own, and happily recommended more. They encouraged me to write
new stories, while at the same time offering detailed
and unflinching critiques of what I had written, honor-
ing my intention to become a writer by offering critical

resistance (this resistance is a large part of the student-mentor equation). The support I received from these teachers struck the perfect balance of rigor and generosity. They took me seriously and—I must repeat—all during their free periods, at lunch, and in after-school talks, *on their own time.*

One of the structural changes in high school that allowed for such intense and durable mentoring was the simple fact that I was a student there for four years. Out of this continuity my most important student-mentor relationship unfolded.

In junior high I had made the rather uninformed choice to study French—it seemed "sophisticated"—instead of the much more California-appropriate Spanish, and at Branham I continued this study because it seemed easier than starting a whole new language. Branham had only one French teacher, and for four years running, one hour a day, and many more after school, I studied with Sally Galbraith, Miss G., Mademoiselle G.

Branham was Miss G.'s first teaching assignment, which would have made her twenty-three or twenty-four, not that many years older than her oldest students. We liked that; she could "relate" to us, we undoubtedly said back then. She was shorter than most of us, feisty and funny, a tad profane, and yes, she did relate to us, but she combined this intimacy with a demanding scholarship.

I had always been a reasonable student in English, articulate in class, if a little too willing to articulate, and in junior high, simply because I spoke often and was good at faking it, I found myself tracked into advanced English classes, where we read books and talked about them, but learned nothing of grammar, syntax, or even the parts of speech. I have never diagrammed a sentence in my life. Miss G. spent a good deal of time engaging us in conversational French, but as much time introducing us to the most basic elements of language. What I know about English sentences and the construction of them, I learned from the study of French. As friendly as she was, Miss G. never stopped pointing to the blackboard, keeping us focused on our subject.

Those of us who persevered with French over those four years grew close as a group, seated in the same classroom every day for four years. French I had its own class periods, but in French II, III, and IV, as some students dropped the language, we shared the same class period. Miss G. knew that students could learn from one another, so she grouped us in conversation pairs, where we practiced our halting, imperfect sentences: *Où est la bibliothèque? La bibliothèque est là-bas.* She helped us to learn on our own by asking us to teach others. In French III and IV, I taught small groups of French II students, and learned even more about grammar from that exercise. When you have to describe something to another, you know it better for yourself. Teaching, Miss G. understood, was a great way to learn.

Miss G. also understood the power of peers to influence a student. By my sophomore year, Miss G. and I had forged a close relationship, and she was quite aware of my inability to "apply" myself, as the report cards said semester after semester. She also knew, from my extra-curricular conversations with her, that my life outside school had taken a troubling direction—she was constantly hectoring me to stop getting stoned. So, quite explicitly, she teamed me on several projects with Jeff Jacobson, a fellow sophomore.

Jeff was a "brain." He got As in everything, each A seemingly effortless; to my eye, he was a genetically superior thinker. But Jeff had transferred to Branham from a private school "back east," where he had received a more directed scholastic training than most of us public school kids. He wasn't snooty about it, far from it; he was generous. Jeff's influence on me, all funneled through Miss G.'s class structure, was sharp and lasting.

After several weeks of working together, Jeff uttered a simple sentence that really did change my life—though again, school had been preparing me to take advantage of this "lightning" moment. Jeff and I were leaving Miss G.'s class one day, after slogging through the French subjunctive, when Jeff turned to me and said, "You know, you're really smart, and if you tried just a little bit, put in a *little* effort, you'd get straight As." That was all he had to say. He went off to his next class, I to mine. What Jeff told me seems nearly offhand now, but it struck a chord that resonated. And on a merely practical level, straight As seemed a good idea, if only to get everyone off my back.

I began to put in more effort after that day—completing assignments, keeping up with the reading, that's about it, nothing as active as extra credit or tutors or the like. By the end of the year, I was getting some As, and for the next two years—with just a *little* effort, mind you—I got nothing but As. My thanks are due to Jeff, but also to Miss G., who knew that sometimes the teacher has to step out of the way.

There was also the friendship Miss G. offered me. A truly committed teacher, she was invested in the whole student and claimed a stake in my life that went beyond test scores. Miss G. and I spent time, both in and after class, talking about, plainly put, Life. A teenager has quite a life to talk about, dramas of any number and variety—love life or the lack of it, home life, weighty thoughts about reality and one's place in it. Miss G. never failed to take me seriously. This is what great teachers do, even while they might be dismissing—read, putting into perspective—a specific problem (no, breaking up with your girlfriend is *not* the end of the world). I was never Miss G.'s friend; I remained her student, but she was my friend and confidant. And so I confided in her. What that means to a teenager: being heard.

During our four years together there were many occasions when Miss G. and I, and the other French students, went off-campus together: foreign language fairs, film festivals, and one memorable dinner at Chez Yvonne (escargot and flaming desserts). On the night we went to Chez Yvonne, the class carpooled, and I ended up—I think by my design—driving home with Miss G. in her Audi, the last to be dropped off. For a long time we sat in her car in front of my house, talking

about, well, it was something important, or perhaps a
string of unimportant things, but a far-ranging conversation nonetheless. I believe I did most of the talking,
Miss G. most of the listening.

I imagine that today, nearly forty years later, such
conversations—teacher and student alone in a car at
night—are forbidden, certainly frowned upon. And
probably with good cause. But I hope innocent moments can still occur between a teacher and a student.
As my sense of myself and the world expanded, and
as I went more widely into the world, led there by my
school and my teachers, one valuable lesson that stayed
with me is that I could connect with people who were
not my peers, could connect with adults in meaningful
and important ways.

I will not lie: I did have something of a romantic
crush on Miss G., but that is to be expected. Teaching
is an intimate act, and that intimacy can become con-
fused in the student's mind with other visions of intimacy. But Miss G., as good teachers know they must,
simply ignored my crush on her and reinforced the
necessary boundaries, all so that she could remain my
confidant.

I do recall that Miss G. and I talked about Paris that
night, about the possibility of my going there someday.
She told me of her visits to France, the thrill of them,
and that night in the car, my teacher and confidant
convinced me I could actually go there someday; that
if I, yes, applied myself, I could do what I wanted to
do, maybe even discover new things I didn't yet know

I wanted to do. Miss G. taught me everything I would
ever need to know about irregular verbs, but as with all
the best teachers, she taught me more than facts; she
taught me how to think about the world, about what I
knew and didn't know, and how I might better become
a part of that world. As with all the best teachers, from
here I learned not *what* to think as much as *how*. Or
as Jim Harrison writes, from a slightly different angle,
"Nearly everything we are taught is false / except how
to read"—how to read books and how to read the world.

I did eventually go to Paris, though not for many
years. Miss G. and her conjugation lessons followed me
everywhere on that trip, as if perched on my shoulder,
still teaching me. At the end of the trip, I wrote her a
letter from a grungy *tabac* on rue de Rivoli, thin blue
airmail stationery crabbed with sentences in passable
French about all I had seen—Dublin, Oxford, London,
Florence, Vienna, Paris. I mailed it across the ocean, a
missive from the far-flung world.

I don't think it's a stretch to say that without the change
of course my high school and its teachers provided, I
might never have gone to Europe on my own, might
instead have led a life that stalled in San Jose, a more
insular and less engaged life, and in the worst-case sce-
nario, an impoverished and imprisoned life. Certainly,
I would not have gone to university were it not for the
support my high school provided; for me, university
proved a surprising and essential place, one that pushed
me both farther and further into the world, per school's

most basic intentions and designs. And I was not alone in my luxurious fortune. While I did know a few fellow students who got lost—into drugs, poverty, prison— there were many others, like me, who were given the opportunity to find a new, expanded, and engaged life for themselves. Most of us at Branham not only survived but also thrived. What's surprising, if anything, about my story is that it is a common one: I was a failing student who, because of the *everyday* workings of my high school, was given a chance at redemption. Yes, I had to make the choice myself, but school made that choice visible to me.

Independent Study

It seemed only natural after visiting my K–12 schools, and having embarked on an investigation of what happens *essentially* in those classrooms, that I should continue my journey with a visit to the colleges I attended—and there were several. But I did not feel compelled to visit those campuses in order to reconstruct them. Perhaps this was because the engines of memory, revved up by my visits to Bagby and Price and Branham, were now fully under way, so I had no need to see the schools physically. They were already vivid to me.

Or perhaps I didn't have to visit these schools because of certain qualities specific to the institution itself. Centuries older than K–12, the university is necessarily a more diverse institution, less uniform in its pedagogies and more ragged in its structures. College is bound to be a more idiosyncratic experience than kindergarten because colleges themselves tend to be less alike than K–12 schools, and their students, too, tend to be less alike.

But maybe there is a more obvious reason I didn't
need to visit those campuses. I hold my college years in
a different part of my memory, nearer and more readily available. College is not tied to my long-gone child
self and the deeper pockets of my past. When I went
to college, I was an adult, and had begun to put into
practice the unique combination of ideas and skills my
earlier education had instilled in me. I was more fully
formed—or so I wanted to believe—by the time I went
to college. I had left home.

School, if pursued long enough, eventually fulfills
its promise of expansion and invites the student to leave
home. For years our teachers pointed to the blackboard
and what lay beyond it, asking us to imagine ourselves
there. We take tentative first steps. Many of us go "off"
to college, "away" to university.

When Maddy first started preschool, a fellow parent
asked me, quite earnestly, what college I had in mind
for her, a question I found absurd. Maddy had yet to say
whether she even wanted to go to college; three-year-
olds can be coy that way. College has become the un-
questioned goal for the "successful" student and her
family, a last station of certificates that promises long-
term economic surety. But when I decided to go to
college, it was naively, simply for the fun of it, for continuing my studies. Reading books and talking about
them, living on my own—of a fashion—and following
some dream of being a writer, it all sounded good to me.
College seemed merely the great luxury that it can be.

There was another fortuitous accident, once again prompted by my high school's structures, that made me understand college was something I might do, could do, should do. In the spring of my junior year, Branham held several college "fairs," with representatives from various schools coming to campus to pass out colorful brochures and talk up their programs. What enticed me about the fair was a simple but ironic factor: you got out of class if you went. In the cafetorium I listened to eight presentations, then wandered from table to table and spoke with school representatives. The admissions directors of St. John's in New Mexico and Occidental College in Southern California, after learning of my recent academic success, both encouraged me to apply; they told me I was just the kind of student they were looking for. Whether they said this to everyone or not, I can't be sure, but their encouragement got my brain clicking.

The following week I met with Branham's own college counselor, who also said I might do well in college. Mrs. Wilson helped me set an application schedule, introduced me to the shelves of resource materials in her office, and by fall term of my senior year, I'd taken the SAT (scores: not bad, not great), completed my required classes, and applied to five schools. Against the odds, I was off to college.

Bologna is often considered the first university in Europe, the genesis of a long tradition that remains unbroken. The university at Bologna may have started as early as

1090, but by the end of the twelfth century, it was a thriving center of learning that drew students from all over the continent.

It's interesting to note that, in an era when the church held sway over every aspect of life and thought, Bologna's university was founded not as a school of theology but a school of law. Europe was rising out of its Dark Ages, the economy recovering from centuries of depression, its society evolving from brute feudalism into a more urban, skill-centered marketplace. People gravitated to cities for the opportunity to learn new crafts under the umbrella of guilds and other civic bureaucracies, and with these more secular complexities came a need for laws, and for those who could read, write, and interpret the laws.

In Bologna, however, and elsewhere, the appearance of the university was not a sudden thing. Small, private schools, usually led by one teacher, first arose to meet the needs of the newly thriving cities, and these schools eventually allied with one another, forming colleges, or "faculties." The colleges soon combined to form a university, and this definition remains with us: a college contains a single scholarly discipline; a university collects many colleges. By 1400 Bologna contained four colleges: law, theology, medicine, and the arts. The arts included philosophy, astronomy, and rhetoric, similar to those colleges we call arts and sciences today.

By the end of the twelfth century, universities had been established in Oxford and Paris, and in the thirteenth century in Cambridge and Montpellier. By 1400 there were universities throughout Italy and Spain, and in Prague, Vienna, and Krakow; by 1500 there were some eighty universities across Europe.

Like today's college freshmen, medieval university students mostly lived in residence halls leased by the university, though these were often scattered about the city. Classrooms might be scattered, too, and because the accretion of schools into a university was haphazard at first, there was often no central campus, as we now expect. Medieval residence halls were often unheated and underfurnished, their residents undernourished. A scholar's life in this era was often a rather ascetic one. And though I would hardly describe today's college students as monkish, there remains a certain material impoverishment that seems inherent in college life.

Early university teachers frequently lived in these dormitories, too, though sometimes students lived in the homes of their teachers, working off their tuition and keep through household chores. These students might be as young as twelve or thirteen, so such supervision seems a good idea. Today, such supervision still seems necessary. College is not a home but a way station, dorm life merely a bridge between childhood and the "real" world, with students in need of a last bit of hand-holding while they first spread their often clumsy and impetuous wings.

Though I was following a centuries-old path when I went off to college, I chose a school that was, at least in its campus and quality of life, more luxurious than

anything a twelfth-century Bologna freshman could
have imagined.

The University of California at Santa Barbara, a few
hours north of Los Angeles on a long stretch of Pacific
beach and cliff, resembles a resort more than a monas-
tery. In the size and suburban layout of the campus, it
seemed to me a natural evolution of the other California
public schools I had attended. While UCSB sported mod-
ernist 1960s cubes, some low, peaked roofs still were evident, along with vast quads and playing fields.

UCSB first opened in 1891 as a teacher's college, but in
1944 it became the third of what are now ten University
of California campuses, a system with an enrollment
of over two hundred thousand. Operated under the
aegis of the state of California, the UC system is supported, in large part, by taxpayer dollars. California
also supports a parallel system, the California State
University, twenty-three campuses with more than
four hundred thousand students. The major difference
between the two systems, other than one of perceived
prestige—UCs are thought of as "harder" schools—is
one, literally, of degrees. UCs may confer PhDs, while
CSUs typically offer only master's degrees. Research is
also a priority at UCs, while CSUs focus on instruction.

In 1862, Congress approved the Morrill Act, offering
federal land grants to individual states for the purpose
of building publicly supported colleges. The original
intention of these land grants was the establishment
of technical colleges, with an emphasis on agriculture.
These more vocational schools, though, soon added

general curricula, often absorbing existing "normal," or teacher-training, colleges already funded by state monies. By the middle of the twentieth century, each of the fifty states boasted one or more tax-supported university or college systems.

The long-swelling tide of education continued: more schools for more students.

I undoubtedly chose to go to UCSB for all the wrong reasons, the first of which was that it seemed like a fun place, with a reputation as something of a party school. But it was also an academically rigorous school, which I learned on my first trip to the campus bookstore, where I bought a stack of seven books for one class's ten-week quarter. It was clear I was meant to study here.

I had no idea at the time, nor would I have as my college life progressed, how higher education might benefit my "career" or "lifetime earning potential." I was lucky enough to be naive about such matters. I went to college, instead, for the simplest reasons, reasons that rarely seem to concern us any longer. I went to college to learn about the world, to "better" myself, for the edification it offered, and because, most importantly, learning still delighted me. The simple wonder of learning new things about the world, inculcated in me in kindergarten and fostered all along, had never left. I had faltered in junior high and high school, yes, but that sense of delight had never actually deserted me. And when school did save me, that delight resurfaced. I went to college because I wanted to study, and because school seemed a worthwhile human endeavor, a purpose of its own.

So there I was, overlooking the ocean in my educational paradise, studying Western civ, Greek drama,
advanced French, the Russian novel, film history, astronomy, whatever else I could fit into my schedule. Yes, I'd
left home, but I remained childish in a fashion, learning
because it delighted me. Because it was such a luxury.

But the truth is, a hundred or even fifty years earlier, I
never would have been able to attend college, much less
finish high school. My grandfather was an unschooled
sharecropper, my father only graduated from seventh
grade, and neither of my older siblings went directly to
college. We were a working-class family without the
money for a private university or even the first thought
of attending one. But there I was, a college kid, one big
rung up the social and economic ladder. Again, I was
no exceptional case: 80 percent of the students from my
high school went on to some form of higher education,
and over 50 percent to a university. Most of the schools
we attended were publicly funded.

In 1976, after my freshman year, I left UCSB and returned to San Jose, fruitlessly chasing my high school
girlfriend. As a way of saving money and figuring out
which four-year school I wished to graduate from, I
spent my sophomore year at West Valley Community
College, a sprawling campus in the foothills of the
Santa Cruz Mountains (of course it was sprawling, this
was California). West Valley is a "junior" college, one of
many in a state-supported system that underwent rapid
growth in the 1950s and 1960s.

Junior colleges had first been proposed as early as 1850 by college administrators in Michigan and Minnesota who believed too much of a university's resources were expended on lower-division courses. But the idea didn't take full flight until 1892, when William Rainey Harper, president of the University of Chicago, divided that school into a "university" or "senior" college, and an "academic" or "junior" college. This system gained wide acceptance, but until the second half of the twentieth century, the majority of junior colleges remained private.

But as education became more compulsory and more effective, a new need arose, one that junior colleges were able to fill. Students who would not normally attend college after high school could focus their studies for two years and then transfer to a university, a vital bridge offered to low-income and late-starting students. Students were no longer fated by their high school tracks.

There was also a pressing need at the time for a skilled work force that wasn't necessarily bound for the ivory tower, hence the advent of the A.A. degree, or associate of arts, in disciplines ranging from law enforcement to landscape gardening. As the scope of the junior college's curriculum widened, so did the scope of the students it drew. Beginning in the 1950s, junior colleges really became "community" colleges, as they're most often called now. Older, "returning" students, could attend classes, not to pursue a degree, but simply for the enrichment—art, languages, sciences, wine tasting, photography, anything and everything.

By the middle of the twentieth century, over half of

all U.S. college students had attended junior college at some point. Through the 1950s and 1960s, a new public junior college was built in the United States, on average, once every week. West Valley was one of those colleges; the tuition for the full-time year I spent there was twenty-four dollars.

My lucky streak with teachers continued through my college years, and nowhere was my good fortune more evident than at West Valley. Jerry Crandall, my Brit lit professor for a year—"from Beowulf to Virginia Woolf"—crammed my head with plays and prose, and oh, the poetry. Chaucer's prologue to *The Canterbury Tales* still springs unbidden from me at times in rusty Middle English. Jerry Crandall was a brilliant teacher, passionate and learned. No, he was not the leading critic in his field, but this was all to my advantage. Instead of revolutionizing critical theory, he was teaching.

Mathematically challenged as I was, yet requiring a science class, at West Valley I enrolled in Physics for Poets, which sounded pretty easy. The instructor was a tiny man with thick glasses, short curly hair, who wore, yes, a pocket protector in his plaid shirt. He was a soft spoken but compelling lecturer. Search as I have, I cannot remember nor find his name. I wish I could locate him, though, to offer my thanks, because—once again—a teacher, an unexpected one, radically changed how I thought about the world.

Physics for Poets met in one of the science labs—test tubes and beakers and the like—so it all felt very scientific. The course materials, however, spoke differently. We read Madeleine L'Engle's time-travel classic *A Wrinkle in Time* (which I'd first encountered in sixth grade), Lewis Carroll's reality-bending *Alice's Adventures in Wonderland* and *Through the Looking Glass,* and Edwin Abbott's inter-dimensional mathematics fantasy *Flatland.* But we also had a physics textbook that was all science and no litera-ture. This was metaphorical teaching at its finest; our teacher guided us down unknown avenues by compar-ing them to those we had already walked. Literature led us to physics.

It was the tests in this class, however, that offered the most valuable instruction. And shouldn't that be what a test is, more teaching than evaluation, a challenge rather than a conclusion?

Each test that semester was simple: twenty true/false statements. But instead of judging the statements true *or* false, we had to prove each one true, using a law of physics; then we had to prove the same statement false, using a different law of physics.

Here is an example of such a test, which I've been able to re-create with the help of Dr. Richard Piccioni of the Bay School of San Francisco.

Statement: Potential energy is stored energy.

T: The potential energy of a system comprising a book and the earth is increased by the work done in lifting the book. That work increases

system potential energy, which remains
available for later transfer to the system's
surroundings.

F: The potential energy of a spinning flywheel is
the same as a stationary one, yet slowing the
spinning flywheel will result in the immediate
transfer of energy to the surroundings, either
by heat or by work.

Physics for Poets taught me the laws of motion and
thermodynamics, but also exposed me to this startling
knowledge: something can be both true *and* false at the
same time. For instance, when recently discussing a
Civil War homework assignment with Maddy, we decided together that the United States was a land of both
great freedom and great enslavement.

Textbooks aside, Physics for Poets costs me all of two
dollars.

After that year, I left West Valley for Santa Clara
University, only a twenty-minute drive away (though
I was back in the Santa Clara Valley of my childhood,
I had left home all the same, living on my own and
working nearly full-time for that privilege). The Jesuits
founded SCU in 1851, which makes it the oldest college
in California. While it predates the suburban schools
of my youth, the Santa Clara campus was still surpris-
ingly familiar: vast playing fields and low shaded walkways, though with a touch of Spanish mission–style
architecture.

I had never considered a private school, public school student that I was, but my education in public schools had offered me enough of an advantage that I found myself with a full-tuition academic scholarship at Santa Clara. I was no genius, simply one more student on the way up, offered a chance at higher education, a chance that felt quite rare but was in fact quite common.

Through all of these different types of schools, I continued to experience the social expansion that school may introduce. I met trust-fund babies and students who worked two and three jobs just to take the minimum load; international students, GI Bill vets, working moms, retirees, and the usual suspects, those kids who went to college because it was what you did. School takes us, as I've said, both farther and further, if only within the classroom.

At West Valley I frequently found myself in the classic classroom, rows of desks aimed at a blackboard. One difference, though, was the transitory nature of the classes, each class scheduled for a given room at a certain time, two or three days a week. As a result, the classrooms were bare. No teacher's personally appointed desk, no posters, no student artwork, no hamsters in cages. Students and teacher gathered for one or two, sometimes three hours; we focused on our subjects, expanded our questions, then departed for another anonymous classroom.

But college also offered two types of classroom that were unfamiliar to me, the lecture hall and the seminar room. Each of these classrooms, because of how it is configured, how it approaches the questions of focus and expansion, is crucial to higher learning.

At UCSB, my Western civ classroom was a five-hundred-seat lecture hall, with a raised stage and an array of screens and overhead projectors. Hundreds of us trooped in every other day for lectures that began the year in ancient Egypt and ended it with Hiroshima. We sat in our seats, took out our notebooks, and scribbled. There was no attendance taken, no questions begged from the back row, no slowing down or going over. If students were noisy in their seats, it was now fellow students who shushed them.

Since UCSB was perched over a beautiful but tar-stained beach, there was always a stack of wet, sand-flecked surfboards near the back door of the lecture hall. Not me, but others would catch waves between classes.

Lecture halls aren't necessarily about cramming as many students into a class as possible. The lecture hall is suited to the sweeping, the overview—Western civ, astronomy, chemistry—the big pictures. The lecture hall is as big as the subject, and grand gestures can be made here.

But as I focused on my major—English, of course, always a wise career choice—I found myself increasingly in the seminar room. Here we return to the university in its primal state, a handful of students gathered around one master, everyone discussing and dissecting the same book. At Santa Clara, appropriately for a Jesuit university, we had rather posh seminar rooms. Each of these rooms had one long wooden table, wood-paneled walls, glass-fronted bookcases. Four or six or eight of us would sit around the table, and with the instructor mediating, dig into what we had read.

It is important in seminar that the instructor mediate rather than lecture. In a seminar students put forth their own ideas, while at the same time listening to and arguing with those of their peers. In a seminar, the subject—the adjectives in Flannery O'Connor's fiction, say—is plumbed far more deeply than in the lecture hall, a focus that is nearly casuistic, the counting of angels on the head of a pin. But such casuistry stems from the expansive subjects we, students and teachers alike, already held in our heads. Because we had expanded our learning so much—we knew the history of civilization!—we were now free to focus ever more narrowly. We were majoring. It is at this point in one's education that, the gross body of knowledge already captured, students begin to add to that body of knowledge with their own discoveries. In a poetry seminar at Santa Clara, one student—a math major!—unlocked a hidden code in a John Donne sonnet that centuries of scholars had missed; her discovery was published in a national literary journal. The student no longer simply listens but speaks.

During my two years at Santa Clara, I began to enroll in independent studies, my first real steps away from the classroom. Santa Clara offered a minor in creative writing, and Jim Degnan was *the* writing teacher, a legend on campus, rarely seen, like the yeti (it's true; today I know SCU English major alums who never once saw him). He was not Professor Degnan, always and only Degnan. The legend of Degnan centered on his toughness, the rigor and workload he demanded of his students. One didn't sign up for Degnan; one submitted to him. In the final weeks of my second quarter at SCU, I placed the draft of a new short story in the box on Degnan's office door, and a week later I was summoned.

The English Department was then housed in a former Jesuit residence hall, and each office retained the patina of monastic life. I had imagined I was signing up for a class, but didn't yet know I had embarked on a new devotion. I knocked on Degnan's heavy oak door, and a drawling voice beckoned. "Enter."

James P. Degnan was tall and thin, and dressed like a secret service agent, skinny black suit, skinny black tie, thick black glasses. He didn't look anything like I imagined writers looked like. He was a good old southern boy, a civil rights Democrat, and a first-generation student of the New Critics. His accent was as thick as, well, butter on grits; he said "otter" space instead of "outer" space. I had been loading up on Faulkner and Welty and Percy, so the accent worked for me.

Like most legends, Degnan was softer in person than in myth. We talked briefly that first day, and he laughed a lot, poking fun at the English Department and the university in general. And he asked me what writers I read. Along with the southern writers, I'd become enamored of Raymond Carver, Stanley Elkin, Donald Barthelme, Joan Didion (the book hunger Mrs. Jouthas unlocked for me in high school had become by now an insatiable appetite). At the end of the meeting, Degnan told me that he would work with me. He thought my story was good enough—"you've a fair hand"—but he was more taken by my reading list. "You read," he said. "None of these other kids read. That's good." We shook on it.

The plan for the course was simple. Every week I was to drop a short story in the box on his door. The following week I would drop off another manuscript, pick up the edited version from the previous week, and get back to work. During a school quarter, I might work on only two stories, but each story went through five or more drafts; one quarter I worked on a single story, though ten complete drafts.

A Degnan-edited manuscript was a bloody battle-field. Red ink spilled across the pages, words and sentences and paragraphs crossed out, arrows overlapping and colliding, and in the margins bold commands and critiques—"awkward," "unclear," "vague," "shallow," with an occasional "lovely" or "nicely done." On the last page of the manuscript, in the same bloody ink, was a direct and clear and concise note intended to lead me deeper into the next draft. Those bloodied manuscripts are long gone, but I vividly remember one phrase: "This doesn't yet read like a Buzbee story." A double-edged sword, that. I was disappointed the draft wasn't working, but for the first time I was given a sense that there might be something someday called a "Buzbee story." Degnan never judged my stories as successes or failures, however; each draft was about the next draft.

Our independent studies, Degnan's method promised, would accompany me beyond graduation, beyond the classroom, out into the world, to the next draft of who I would be.

A couple of times each quarter, I would meet Degnan for a conference in his office, most often in the late afternoons when the campus was eerily quiet. While we did talk about my stories during these conferences, we mostly didn't. We talked about books and writing, in a way I knew even then was intended to offer guidance beyond university requirement. Degnan was generous with his time and his experiences, and I soaked up every word, as a student should. As with my previous mentors, our relationship was a friendly one, but we were never really friends. He remained my mentor. Even years after leaving Santa Clara, when Degnan and I would meet for dinner in San Francisco, everything he said came to me from this understanding: he was ever the teacher, not by force, not by egotism, but by the nature of the unspoken contract we had both agreed to.

Which isn't to say we didn't have a drink or two. One late afternoon early in my apprenticeship, Degnan opened the bottom drawer of his desk and poured us shots of bourbon, a ritual that remained regular. You can only imagine how psyched I was about that—not for the booze, nor the transgression of it, but for the honor of it. It may have been thirst on Degnan's part, but to me it felt like an anointment. Rather than break down the teacher-student contract, those shots of bourbon in many ways affirmed it.

Degnan has remained my teacher since; he sits on my shoulder when I write, his red pen constantly nagging. When I edit student papers and stories today, I use red ink, too. For its visibility, and for its bloodiness, but also for the tradition it preserves, the inheritance. And on occasion, I take my adult students out for a drink, where I tell tales out of school, where I talk to them—in emulation of Degnan—about what comes after the classroom.

By the time I was ready to graduate from Santa Clara, it was too late for me: I'd become a confirmed student, one desirous of education's luxuries, and I now thrived on school. As graduation approached, I was offered a well-paying position "writing" technical manuals for government-contracted weapons systems, but thanks to the English and writing teachers I'd encountered over the past eight years, this "real" job had no appeal for me. I wasn't sure what I wanted to do exactly, except that I wanted to keep my devotion to writing and was not yet ready to give up my college-supporting job in bookselling, which had become a devotion of another kind, one verging on a career. When in doubt, apply to graduate school.

The spring of my senior year, I stumbled on a classified ad in the *New York Review of Books* for the Goddard College Low-Residency MFA Program for Writers. The ad listed the short story writer Raymond Carver as one of the faculty; a few years before I'd fallen under Carver's spell, and so I applied to this program I knew very little about. I wasn't at all clear on the concept of low-residency learning, so that summer when I flew to Montpelier, Vermont, to begin the program, I left the return portion of my ticket open-ended.

Goddard's MFA program was started in 1976 by the poet Ellen Bryant Voigt, who, discouraged by the harsh and competitive atmosphere she found at the famed Iowa Writers' Workshop, wanted to create an alternative to the traditional workshop model. Many MFA students, Voigt knew, were older, established in homes and careers, and so moving to Stanford or Iowa or New York City was out of the question. The slow study and practice of writing, she knew, did not depend on thrice-weekly class meetings. Why couldn't writers study one-on-one with more mature writers, a method of mentoring that had been practiced informally for thousands of years? And why couldn't you just stay home and write?

By the 1970s Goddard already offered low-residency studies for undergraduates, and using this model, Voigt proposed her MFA program. She assembled a young but impressive faculty—Louise Glück, Heather McHugh, Stephen Dobyns, Raymond Carver, Thomas Lux, Michael Ryan, to name only a few—and set off into the unknown. In 1980, with Goddard College undergoing a series of financial setbacks, Voigt and the program relocated to Warren Wilson College in North Carolina, and it is now one of the most highly regarded writing programs in the United States. Its low-residency format is no longer an anomaly; today there are at least thirty-seven such programs.

In the low-residency format, students and faculty are not required to move to campus, or anywhere near it. Twice a year, students and faculty converge on the campus for a ten-day "residency," living in dorms, taking classes, conducting workshops, attending readings, and engaging in less studious high jinks, throwing a dance, swimming naked in Snake Lake, an amorous dalliance here and there. Students and teachers then disperse, returning to wherever it is they live, to begin the six-month semester. Every three weeks or so the student sends off a packet of work, and continues on the next leg of the journey, while waiting for the teacher's lengthy, written response (not all responses to my work were written; one of my instructors, Frank Conroy, dictated his comments on audiocassette, the clink of ice in his scotch audible under his prep school New England drawl).

The financial and structural advantages of a low-residency program are readily apparent. I was able to work full-time and still go to school, without uprooting my life. But the real advantage, at least for me, came with the slow, constant, evolving relationships with my teachers. One-on-one, and only one-on-one, I worked through each semester, and that work was pushed and prodded by my teacher. We worked in silence, far from the bustling campus and the chatterbox of workshop.

At Warren Wilson, I studied one semester each with Frank Conroy, who taught me about the difficulty of creating a "good" sentence; Barbara Greenberg, who made me, almost therapeutically, examine the deep wellsprings of my fictional world; Stephen Dobyns, who, as

he promised, broke me like a pane of glass and transformed me from an enthusiastic reader into a critical one;
and David Huddle, who generously suggested that, yes,
I could write a novel, and guided me through the first
spindly chapters. Each of my teachers was a working
writer: all were teachers, yes, but they were all working on their own writing first; they were writers who
wrote, not writers who had once written.

It was vocational, that instruction. And while these
teachers of mine had other students at other colleges, the
instruction I received from them—a true mentoring—
was in a classroom only I inhabited, my desk at home.
A fully independent study.

When I graduated from Warren Wilson in 1982, school
had finally pushed me back into the world, and I thought
for a long time that I was done with the classroom.

Continuing Education

In an interview shortly before his death in 1991, the writer Isaac Bashevis Singer predicted that in the future everyone would become a graduate student.

Although I'd loved my own graduate studies, at first I found Singer's idea merely amusing. Why would anyone wish to live in such penury while going deep into debt? I took it at face value that Singer was being satirical, but there was a tone to his prediction, both hopeful and sincere, that made me return to his statement from time to time. I now understand, I think, what Singer wished for his fellow humans. If we all were to become perpetual students, not only would the global body of knowledge expand, not only would we find engaged and purposeful lives, but we would all be too busy with our studies to create the kind of havoc that humans are so adept at creating.

Singer's vision is a naive fantasy, impossible but worth considering. As the human experiment with civilization continues, one undeniable constant has been the ever more inclusive classroom. More people receive formal educations today than at any previous time, and even when formal education ends, many graduates choose to remain students. We continue our educations not because we have to but because we want to, not only because it might further our careers but also because it gives us pleasure to be in the classroom and study there some facet of life on the planet. We enter the classroom again because it improves—dare I say it?—the quality of our lives. The adage comes in many forms: one is never too old to learn; one is always a student; the world is a classroom; the unexamined life is an unworthy life.

Today there is an astounding variety of "postgraduate" education available. Such classes are often found in more traditional academic settings—community colleges, university extension programs, various types of "night school." But there are also courses, in every imaginable subject, sprinkled throughout the community in storefronts or living rooms or garages. If you want to learn something, all you have to do, apparently, is raise your hand.

Classes and private instruction are advertised on the bulletin boards of coffee shops, Laundromats, grocers, and in the back pages of free newspapers, or on flyers taped to telephone poles and streetlights.

Here are some classes I found advertised on a recent stroll through my San Francisco neighborhood: Chinese, Russian, Portuguese, French, Italian, Arabic, and English. Piano, Voice, Guitar, Bass Guitar, Woodwinds,

Chinese Instruments. Tai Chi, Karate, Tae Kwon Do, Badminton, Dodgeball, Volleyball, Triathalon. Children's Writing, Novels, Short Stories, Memoir, Screenplay. Life Drawing, Landscape Painting, Chinese Calligraphy. Bonsai, Composting, Succulents. An incredible array of Yogas. Positive Thinking, Meditation. And, yes, even How to Twitter.

Surely there's a class for you.

In *The Triggering Town,* the American poet Richard Hugo advised his writing students to refrain from teaching for ten years after graduation. With writing such a slow art to conquer, or even achieve competence in, how could one go from student to master so quickly? Wasn't a longer apprenticeship required?

When I graduated with my MFA, I did not start sending out teaching CVs; my focus remained on my own writing, though I did hold in the back of my mind the idea that I might enjoy teaching one day. While supporting myself in college, I had stumbled on a career that thoroughly engulfed me, the book business, first as a bookseller and then as a publisher, and I stayed in that world for twelve years after my "terminal" degree, before I finally became a teacher.

I had made an earlier foray into teaching, however. Much as the reading of powerful books had inspired me to try my own hand at writing, so did being the student of great high school teachers—Mrs. Jouthas, Miss Long, Mrs. Weinberg, Mr. Beebe, Miss Galbraith—inspire me to think of being a great high school teacher myself, to repay what I thought of as my debt to them. It's a common story, this, teachers entering the profession because of the example of their own teachers. I had also believed—quite wrongly—that the life of a high school teacher might mix well with that of a writer, summers off and all that. So during my senior year at Santa Clara, I took two courses in the Education Department while concurrently teaching two courses as a student teacher in the nearby public high school.

I was assigned to English classes, naturally, and in each I worked under an experienced teacher. I read and graded student papers, and once or twice a week I would lead the daily lesson, but most often I sat in the back of the classroom and observed. What I saw from this vantage—two completely different types of teachers—made me realize that if I were going to be a high school teacher, I needed to be a fully dedicated one.

Ms. Pinkton had been teaching high school English for twenty-five years, and was, although well intentioned, clearly burned out. During our first conference she gave me the lowdown on her students, which students received which grades. When I read the first batch of papers, though, it was clear to me that Ms. Pinkton no longer "saw" her students. One of her D students wrote an inspired critique of Poe's "The Fall of the House of Usher." The paper had a few grammatical issues, but these were easily corrected. One of her A students, however, wrote a paper that, while "correct" in most ways, was quite dull, a paper aimed at pleasing the teacher. I don't blame Ms. Pinkton for her fatigue; teaching, especially grades K–12, is rigorous and exhausting work, and not everyone is suited to it.

Mr. Carlo, on the other hand, was dynamic and energetic, engaged with his students at every level of their lives. Mr. Carlo's classes were loud and kinetic, by design, and every day—I do mean every single day—called for a new approach, a new strategy. Not just new content, but different approaches to that content that would ensure the students were fully engaged each time they entered the classroom. When Mr. Carlo sat me down to discuss "our" students, he didn't tell me which grades they got, but instead talked to me about the strengths and weaknesses of each, and asked me to brainstorm different methods of helping them individually. I was astonished to discover how much he knew about the home and personal lives of his charges, how much he worked with them outside classroom concerns. While I studied under Mr. Carlo that semester it became evident that teaching was his life, and that his evenings and his weekends were consumed by his classes and his students.

When my high school teachers invested so much of themselves in me, I took this attention for granted (though not without gratitude), unable, from deep in my teenage tunnel, to consider how many other students they helped in the same ways, and how draining that might be. *Consuming,* that is the proper word. During my semester of student teaching, I realized that if I were to become the kind of teacher I aspired to—a truly effective teacher, an *important* one—I would have to devote myself to the task without reservation, and there would be no room for a writing life. It's no wonder Frank McCourt—by all accounts a very important teacher to hundreds of students—had to wait until his career was ending to write *Angela's Ashes*. He had neither the time nor energy to get it done before that. And so, somewhat disappointed in myself, I stepped away from teaching. I selfishly chose writing instead.

When the next opportunity to teach arrived, it was something of an accident. Having published a first novel—"to howls of neglect," as Brian Eno said of one his albums—I decided in 1993 to leave the book business and pursue my writing with greater diligence. I had enough savings to hold me for a year, was going to sell that second novel, write a third, and then, well, I was a little hazy about the future, but surely something would turn up (as a devoted English major, farsighted career decisions have never been my forte). But a week after I gave notice at Chronicle Books, Liz McDonough called me out of the blue and offered me the chance to teach a class at the UC Berkeley Extension. An instructor scheduled for the upcoming term had backed out, Liz heard I had published a novel, and she was a bit desperate.

A few weeks later I was on the Berkeley campus, at seven o'clock at night, standing in front of a room full of strangers, a blackboard behind me. I had, of course, so overprepared that first session that I barely got through half of my notes before the three hours were up. I had no idea what I was doing, but everyone stayed that evening, all evening, and they came back the following week, and the weeks after that. On my way home that first night, I whispered to myself, "Well, I guess you're a teacher," thrilled as much by that idea as by the notion that, with more experience, I might be able to give my students some little bit of what my teachers had given me, might begin to repay that debt. It's twenty years later, and I'm still teaching, still trying to give back.

In 1891 professors from the University of California's original Berkeley campus offered a series of college-level lectures to the adult populace of San Francisco. Each week, these professors would board the ferry and travel across the bay, extending the boundaries of the Berkeley campus (hence the term *extension*) not only geographically but in terms of the student body as well.

The initial lectures developed into short, noncredit, evening courses, the range of courses widened, and the students continued to come. Today UC Berkeley Extension offers fifteen hundred courses a year, on campuses scattered around the Bay Area, in San Francisco and Berkeley, and the outlying suburbs, Los Altos, Marin, San Ramon, etc. Many of the courses in Extension's catalog further one's career development, from AA and Other Mutual Help Groups for Counselors to Zero Net Energy Building. But many of the courses are simply for personal edification: writing, art, gardening, wine tasting. From Harvard to UCLA, many colleges and universities provide such "extension" learning.

What I loved most about teaching at Extension was

the haphazard makeup of each class. Students had only
to sign up, on a first-come, first-served basis, and their
checks (quite small checks) had to clear. There were
usually no other requirements. In any given class I
might have a precocious high school student or two,
along with an array of working folk in their twenties,
thirties, and so on, all the way up to retirees in their
seventies, and on occasion, a feisty ninety-year-old. The
first session of a class was always surprising, and de-
lightfully so, because I never knew who would show up
and say, "Teach me."

At Extension I taught beginning and intermediate
fiction writing, and so there was one common factor
that brought these people to the classroom: they loved
to read. At some point, everyone who loves to read,
whether they admit it or not, thinks, *Oh, I bet I could write
something.* This is a more than reasonable expectation.
One thing about the art of writing is that those who
are "fans" of it, that is, readers, are also equipped with
the basic skills to produce the art they consume. Music
lovers don't always play an instrument, nor museum-
goers paint. Perhaps this explains, a little menacingly,
why NASCAR is so popular: we all drive. Readers already have the tools to write; writing is a democratic
art form.

At the beginning of each course, I would go around
the room and ask everyone why he or she had joined
the class. Each student answered in the same way: *I've
always been a reader, and I just thought . . .* Some students
had written when they were younger, only to have

that fall away when careers and families intervened. On occasion, a student would tell the class a careless (and surely bitter) teacher or other adult had destroyed her confidence with a single damning phrase—"you'll never be a writer"—and it took that student years to regain the courage to try again. A few students had already written a great deal; most had written nothing since getting out of school.

Every week for ten weeks, I gathered my students in one type of classroom or another; Extension makes use of many different sites. There were classrooms on the Berkeley campus, and at Extension's own small campus in San Francisco, itself a former elementary school, and others at high schools and elementary schools during the evening hours when they go unused, and occasionally underused corporate meeting rooms. It's amazing how little it takes to create a classroom: table, chairs, blackboard—done. In Bangladesh's floodplains, classes are often held on wooden boats that travel from village to village; in India, there are classes held under highway overpasses, the concrete walls serving as ad hoc blackboards. Gathered together in a room with a book, as simple as that.

In these Extension classes we talked about the books we were reading, read and discussed student writing, and I pointed to the blackboard. Most of my students worked full-time, had families and friends and other markers of a demanding life, yet they managed to come out once a week, from seven to ten in the evening, for a class that offered nothing but what it offered: the chance to focus and expand. People enrolled because they craved something in their lives beyond work and recreation.

When the master painter and painting teacher Wayne Thiebaud was asked in an interview why art classes were so popular today, his answer was simple: art is a human endeavor. There was nothing about art, he went on, that could be improved by technology, no short-cuts offered through machines; art was a one-on-one struggle, one student wrestling with one task. No matter the subject, be it art or even computing, learning is a human endeavor, a worthwhile and essential pursuit for both student and teacher.

Every year or so, a rather contentious and snarky article, with a title something like "Can Creative Writing Be Taught?," is published to some national attention, sparking heated electronic debates, at least for the seven or so minutes such debates last. The author of this article is always a published writer who feels compelled to rail against writing classes in general, with a special dose of spite reserved for graduate programs in writing, the MFA. The author is often a teacher of writing him- or herself, but one who clearly doesn't enjoy the job. To which I offer the poet Carolyn Kizer's advice: if you don't like to teach, don't; there are easier ways to make money.

The argument of this essay is simple yet sweeping. Writing classes, the author insists, dilute rather than enhance the literature by convincing "everyone" that she or he can write. The charges continue: MFA programs in particular are guilty of encouraging homogeneous, dull, uninspired literature; the ivory tower is bland and tame, whereas "real" writers need "real" life to inspire them (as if the classroom exists outside history, weather, or gravity); the teaching of writing, it is claimed, dulls the sensibilities of those writers who must teach. Writing, the essay suggests, is a type of magic, a birthright, and you've either got it or you don't (inevitably, the author of the essay has got that magic). The essay says to all would-be writers, don't even try.

Allow me to offer an opposing view.

Can creative writing be taught? Of course it can. And it should be. Every subject should be taught. What can be the harm in any continuing education?

For the past fourteen years I've been on the faculty of the MFA program at the University of San Francisco, an intense and expensive two-year course of study. Our students pony up $38,000 (mostly borrowed through student loans and paid back over ten years) for the privilege of spending two nights a week in a classroom after a long day of working full-time jobs, or even more arduously, managing households and families. They give up their other evenings, their weekends, their summers, and their friends, so that they can read and write under deadlines we impose. And they do this despite the fact that we tell them, even before they're admitted, that an MFA degree will not land them a job, nor will publication, and its mythical fame and glory and riches, necessarily follow. You write, we tell our students, because you love to do it, because you have to. Because, no matter the outcome, it is a worthwhile pursuit.

Our MFA students leave with a mountain of debt, a finished and publishable book-length manuscript, and a practice and habit that may follow them into the "real" world. But even the student who never writes again—whether a continuing ed student or an MFA candidate—has had a worthwhile experience encompassing years of engagement with a meaningful human subject. The student is now a better reader of literature, and will have joined, in a material fashion, the literary community at large. Most importantly, though, the student will have created, no matter its "quality" or "success," a testimony to one life as it is lived on our planet.

Let me paraphrase the much-loved writing teacher Linda Palmer of UCLA Extension: I have yet to find a student who didn't have some strength, some spark. Why shouldn't teachers seek out and fan those sparks to whatever flame resides there?

Yes, creative writing can be taught. And it should continue to be taught.

In twenty years of teaching, I've had well over six hundred students, and if I were to count writing conferences and one-time classroom visits, that number would surely be over a thousand. Many of my former students have gone on to publish stories and novels, a couple of them more successful in their writing careers and their art than I can yet lay claim to. This is a risk when you teach writing, or any subject, for that matter, that your students will exceed you. But that risk is also a reward.

My greatest rewards as a teacher, however, remain

the small ones, those moments when a student says, *aha!* A few months after an Extension course in which we read Faulkner's *Absalom, Absalom*, I received a note from a woman who had done nothing but complain about Faulkner the entire time (she was otherwise a lovely student). The note began with her now familiar tirade against Faulkner, but ended with her telling me that finally—*finally!*—she got it; she'd come to understand his rhythms and found herself engaged in all her other reading as she had never been because of reading Faulkner. She had just purchased, she wanted me to know, several others of Faulkner's novels. This I count as the most important kind of victory for a teacher.

If a student is lucky to have one good teacher, then the teacher, too, must have that one good student. I suppose, in a way, that my high school teachers were lucky to have had me for a student once, a student who was ready, primed for the *aha!* moment, who offered a tangible sign to them of their effectiveness, their importance; I'd like to believe that, of course. A teacher teaches to the entire classroom, but depends on one student.

A self-serving reward of teaching, I have come to discover, is that when I teach a novel to my students, I have to teach myself first what that novel is, so I can guide them through it. Joseph Joubert, French educator and essayist, reminds us that "to teach is to learn twice." Teaching makes me smarter.

Last fall I returned to the classroom as a student for the first time in thirty years. I have always admired the fine

arts of drawing and painting, but never once thought I
should pick up a brush. I doodle, but draw? Oh no. My
wife and daughter, however, thought I might need to
get out of the house more often, so they purchased a
class for me as a birthday gift. The class, Everyone Can
Draw, is one of many offered by the Sharon Art Studio,
which is housed in an old brownstone smack dab in the
middle of Golden Gate Park. Each session over six hundred San Francisco residents, adults and kids, sign up
for classes in ceramics, glass, painting, and drawing.

The Sharon Art Studio is a nonprofit organiza-
tion that operates under a lease from the city of San
Francisco. The city is somewhat begrudging in its lease.
Whenever the municipal financial picture is dismal,
as it often is these days, the city threatens to quit the
lease and open a restaurant in the old brownstone. The
building sits on prime real estate at one end of a beautiful meadow directly adjacent to the historic carousel
and children's playground, and only a few minutes'
walk from the tourist destinations of the California
Academy of Sciences and the de Young Museum. I get
it; the restaurant would a big hit, might even bring in
much-needed cash. However, in a city that's besieged by
restaurants, there are a lot of places to eat, but only a few
places in which to learn drawing.

On the first day of Everyone Can Draw, I felt like a
kindergartner again. Coaxed from my home, I set out
with some pencils and a pad, even a snack, and I showed
up in a roomful of strangers, not knowing what to expect but excited to be there. And feeling as vulnerable

as any new student: What if I fail, and fail in front of others? As a longtime teacher, could I be a student again, could I take that risk? But this was school, so familiar to me in its comforts and security that my vulnerability, if not completely calmed, was set to one side, enough to get me started on this new venture.

My classmates and I, adults of all ages and from quite different lives, sat at drawing benches and took out pencils and paper, while the instructor, Virginia Banta, used a blackboard to focus us. She wrote on the board—a good old-fashioned chalkboard—what she hoped to teach, what resources we would need for the journey, how we were to proceed. Then she drew the simple shapes, the ABCs of drawing, that would be our foundation. First a line, then a sphere, then a cone. Back to basics.

I showed up every week for class, did my homework, returned. Every week Virginia used the blackboard to keep us focused. And I learned to draw a little. When the course was over, I'd done passable drawings of a spider plant, the corner of my living room, a cloth draped on an easel, a human face. I will never be an artist, that is not my goal; as Chaucer said, "the lyf so short, the craft so long to lerne." But I went to class, and together with my fellow students, both worked and played.

I have signed up for a second drawing class, confident that what I learned in the first will push me further along. There is Virginia again, at the board, talking to us about perspective. She outlines a landscape for us, talks about the values of shadow and light, the virtues of negative space. But I keep drifting away, to the window next to the blackboard, where eucalyptus trees sway at the far end of the meadow, a hawk wheeling above them, and I see the big world waiting for me out there. Soon, I think, I'll take my pencil and my pad and go out into that world.

Epilogue:
Out of School

I went to school in Paradise.

I was blessed, from kindergarten through grad school, with teachers who were kind to me at the very least, and inspired and inspiring at their very best. My third-grade teacher, Mrs. Bowman, and the large rock she pounded on her desk, was about as cruel a teacher as I ever had, and she was hardly cruel, just a bit grumpy. I was never spoken down to, never discouraged, and when I needed it, found teachers willing to go out of their way to aid me—*yet another student.*

Whether I was merely an average student, as in elementary school, or determined to fail, as in grades eight through ten, or fruitfully engaged, as I was from age fifteen on, there was a steady corps of teachers by my side who helped me focus on the blackboard, and urged me to cast off into the world that waited beyond it. And although I was never exceptional as a student, neither were my teachers or classrooms, at least not in the Hollywood manner. My classrooms were not *To Sir, with*

Love, nor *Dead Poets Society,* nor *Stand and Deliver.* Every generation produces at least one such film, with odds overcome and tearjerking magic created, and ostensibly based on a true story. My teachers and classrooms were only exceptional in that they were exceptionally ordinary. I mean this as the highest praise. School, when it works as we know it can, is more ordinary and available than the movie version. This is school's ultimate triumph, that it is so common.

I'm well aware that I've been studying school often through the naive lens of memory, but the naive lens can be an instructive one, and may allow us to trace the essential shapes of things unmarked by innumerable and distracting details. I might instead have concentrated on public policy or pedagogical methods or textbook content—all pressing and fractious subjects. But I've chosen, until now, to stay in the classroom as much as possible, away from the clamor of that grown-up discourse. I needed to remind myself that, for students, the classroom is where everything happens, or does not. I needed to remind myself of what is possible in the classroom.

But I'm not naive to the obvious reality that school, the classroom, can be for many students a less than desirable way to spend their days. "I hated school," so many people have recently told me (not a few of them, ironically, teachers themselves). I hated school, too, some days.

For centuries, it's true, abuses of various sorts seemed built into the curriculum. One has only to turn to the vast shelf of school memoirs, especially those of British boarding school students, to find vivid portraits of adults' cruelty toward their charges.

George Orwell's classic essay "Such, Such Were the Joys" catalogs an astonishing litany of institutional and individual mistreatment, including horrible food, impoverished living conditions, and "summonses, interrogations, confessions, floggings, repentances, solemn lectures of which one understood nothing."

What Orwell suffered at "Crossgates" included but also went beyond physical pain and privation; the true consequences ran deeper, resulting in

> a deeper grief which is peculiar to childhood and not easy to convey: a sense of desolate loneliness and helplessness, of being locked up not only in a hostile world but in a world of good and evil where the rules were such that it was actually not possible for me to keep them.

Today such practices have been greatly diminished, though not all have been abolished. Students still suffer from physical and mental cruelties, along with even more troubling abuses, at the hands of some, but markedly few, teachers. The ongoing struggle to promote and ensure the safety and well-being of all children continues, as it must, not only at school but in all avenues of life. A good school, a school fully funded and staffed, can, I believe, do much to mitigate the torments a child might suffer there. A *good* school is a place where the child, vulnerable because he or she is a child, should be made to feel secure, comforted, and, from within that security, learn to be adventurous rather than fearful. Better schools create better citizens.

The classroom is not a perfect place. Smaller deficits—if only because they are more prevalent—can make any classroom less than a paradise. As with all occupations, teaching produces its incompetents, and among these, certainly the most pervasive, are boring teachers. And in a time when test scores seem more important than education, the passion to learn can be doused with homework that is both overabundant and superfluous, as well as a focus on standardized performance rather than critical thinking—*what* to learn rather than *how*.

In public schools across the country, teachers are overscheduled, and class sizes are far too large. Students can be overextended, too, tied to academic and extracurricular schedules that rob them of that all-important time for staring out the window. And today's students must cope with a minefield of distractions that might easily derail them: bullying, drugs, gang violence, confusing sexual messages. Previous generations, mine included, also encountered these same distractions, it's true, though it does seem as if they are more pervasive now.

School, though imperfect, is still essential. I'd like to believe that a concerted public focus on what happens *inside* the classroom, rather than what happens in legislatures and on school boards, is the answer to improving our schools, the lives of the children there, and the future we all must share.

School works when given proper conditions. Where would we be without education? To focus on its failures is to lose sight of the immense success of school, all those great teachers, and the very real possibility that any classroom might become a paradise.

Yes, I went to school in paradise, but not one solely of my own good fortune. I was educated during the golden era of the Golden State's commitment to public education, a paradise created for all California students. From kindergarten through high school, as well as in community colleges and state universities, California's public education was, in the decades following World War II, a source of pride and enrichment for the state. I know I'm at risk again of lapsing into nostalgia's glow, but it's a fact that, during my years there, California's school system was ranked number one or two in the nation. Today, depending on the survey, California, the most populous and, by reputation at least, most forward-thinking state in the nation, has fallen to forty-eighth or forty-ninth in academic rankings.

Not long after I graduated from Branham High School, many of the young, idealistic teachers from that school left teaching altogether. Some went into real estate, others into Silicon Valley; one of my favorite history teachers, rather dispiritingly, became a grocery store butcher. When I asked these teachers about their decisions to leave a profession they had trained for and loved, the answer was simple: money. This exodus of skilled teachers might have been a sign of the times, the hopeful 1960s giving way to the more narcissistic 1970s, but the simplest answer shouldn't be avoided: these teachers left because they did not make enough money for the amount of work and responsibility they were asked to undertake. According to Nínive Clements Calegari of the Teacher Salary Project, some 62 percent of today's K–12 teachers need a second job to make ends meet; 46 percent of today's teachers, she says, will leave the profession within their first five years.

The decline in California's public schools has continued, unabated, and today the outlook is grim. The same is true for all other states. Even those states that are now the top rated have suffered steep declines in the amount of money spent annually on each student. Between 2008 and 2013, only Wyoming and North Dakota increased the amount of money spent each year per pupil, but this only after decades of decreasing that amount. California's spending per pupil fell by almost 30 percent during that same time, while Arizona's fell a gut-wrenching 50 percent.

The most basic issue cannot be avoided: money.

Over the fall and winter while I was touring my old schools, my daughter was busily visiting prospective high schools and readying her applications. As a family we had to face again a difficult decision we'd faced twice before, at the beginning of Maddy's elementary and middle schools: public or private?

Though I am the beneficiary of California public schools, Maddy has attended private elementary and middle schools. My wife and I have made these choices not out of the sense that a private school education would better Maddy's chances socially or careerwise, but out of desperation. The public schools in San Francisco are simply too underfunded and overcrowded. Julie and I have debated, over the years, sending Maddy to a public school, sensing that our leaving the public school system could only further diminish it. We've talked of throwing ourselves into those public school communities, as volunteers and fund-raisers, in an effort to improve the schools from within—as many San Francisco parents do.

So when Maddy's high school acceptance letters arrived, we toured the public school she'd been assigned to, a placement many families would have killed for, a college-prep charter school with a fine faculty and sterling reputation. Not only were class sizes enormous and the building—its hallways and classrooms and lunchroom—dilapidated, but the school, while boasting a fine academic program, offered little else apart from the basics required to get a student to college. Art and music and sports and other extracurricular activities were minimal if in place at all. We admired what the school's faculty was doing, but we could not imagine sending Maddy to this impoverished place every day for four years. We decided, selfishly, that we were not willing to sacrifice her education to the outcome of a bake sale.

Again, we must not forget the most basic issue: money. Simply put, state funding is inadequate. In 1977, California spent more money per student than any other state; today it ranks forty-seventh in dollars per student, a number explicitly reflective of its academic standing. Despite a $1 billion Class Size Reduction Initiative, passed in 1996, class sizes in California are on the increase again, in some districts up from twenty to an average of forty students in a classroom. In many of the state's school districts, the number of teaching days per year has been reduced to the barest minimum.

Budget devastation affects not only California's K–12 students but its college students as well. In 2007 a student in the California State University system paid $3,198 in annual tuition and mandatory "campus fees"; for the 2011–12 school year that student paid more than double that amount, $6,422. The number of students admitted to the CSU system will also fall, with an estimated twenty thousand "acceptable" students turned away because budget cuts do not allow for the hiring of enough teachers. At schools in the University of California system, a student paid $13,218 for the 2011–12 year, an 18 percent increase over the previous year, and regents of the university are considering a four-year plan that would increase the annual tuition, campus fees aside, to over $22,000 by 2015. My total tuition for one year at UC Santa Barbara was $800. In all of California's higher education systems—UC, CSU, community colleges—class sizes are increasing, students turned away, faculty let go, courses dropped altogether. In the fall of 2011, for the first time in its history, the UC system received more of its monies from tuition than from the taxpayers of California.

(As I complete the last edits of this book, the state of

California has announced a plan to offer middle-class scholarships to both UC and CSU schools, averaging 30–40 percent of tuition, and based solely on income. This plan is possible because of a surplus of tax revenues, though the tuition hikes remain, as do course cancellations and student population restraints.)

Budget problems, we know, are not confined to California. Nathan Bootz, superintendent of public schools in Ithaca, Michigan, in 2011 begged his governor to turn Ithaca's schools into prisons. Bootz made the following plea to Governor Rick Snyder in a letter published in the local paper:

> The State of Michigan spends annually somewhere between $30,000 and $40,000 per prisoner, yet we are struggling to provide schools with $7,000 per student. I guess we need to treat our students like they are prisoners, with equal funding. Please give my students three meals a day. Please give my children access to free health care. Please provide my school district Internet access and computers. Please put books in my library. ... It's the least we can do to prepare our students for the future ... by [giving] our schools the resources necessary to keep our students OUT of prison.

The above is both a math and an ethics problem.

On June 6, 1978, California voters approved, by a 2 to 1 margin, Proposition 13, the "People's Initiative to Limit

Property Taxation." Prop. 13 rolled back the state's property tax rates, limited future tax increases, and became a
part of the state's constitution, requiring an improbable
number of votes to overturn. The monies from these
property taxes, while they had also supported emergency
and fire services, libraries, and other essential programs,
were the primary source of the bounty that had created
California's public school paradise. The most common
argument in favor of Prop. 13—during the campaign and
in continuing debates today—was a matter of simple,
though I believe shortsighted, greed. My children, voters
said, are no longer in school or are in private school, so
why should I pay for the schools of other people's children? The moment Prop. 13 passed, California's rank
among state school systems began to plummet.

While Prop. 13 was responsible for a severe reversal
in the state's public education system, it was not a singular event, but a bellwether moment. Not long after,
in 1980, Ronald Reagan was elected president, and the
"taxpayer revolt" for which he was the cheerful spokes-
person fully took hold. Since that time, taxes have fallen
in the United States to historically low levels, and today
the call continues from certain, very loud quarters to
keep reducing them.

Class sizes have increased dramatically throughout
the country, while teachers' salaries have fallen in real
terms. In every corner of a school's budget—lunch programs, textbooks, libraries, art and music programs, even
once sacred sports programs—drastic cuts have been

made. The voters have spoken (and make no mistake, *we* are the voters): anything but taxes. Concurrent with this decline in our public education has been a rise in the number of private schools, both for-profit and nonprofit. Those who can afford good schools—or who can, as my family has been able to, find the financial aid—send their children there.

And yet, has there ever been a politician who ran on an "antischool" platform? The public discourse insists that "education" be one of the key planks in any electoral platform. The children are the future, we say blithely and blandly, and we must educate them. America, we say on the campaign trail, must be able to compete in the new global economy, and to do so our children must receive the finest educations available.

Unfortunately, at these same campaign stops, we say—and then vote accordingly—that taxes must never be raised. And so our schools continue to suffer, and if our schools do, so do our students, and if they suffer, then the nation must suffer, too, eventually.

The public will to fund public education remains pallid, timid, hypocritical. We may have standardized tests, computers in every classroom, and stirring speeches from flag-strewn podiums, but these will not compensate for the diminished classroom, the classroom with too many students and not enough teachers.

My tour of school, in both memory and real life, has led me, as school is wont to do, from contemplation to action, from thought to speech. I have to speak up, speak out. The stakes are simply too high to remain silent.

Allow me to digress again, schoolboyishly, aping Jonathan Swift. Here is my *Immodest Proposal* to save our schools:

1. Without qualification, and immediately, halve the student population of every classroom, from forty to twenty, or from thirty-two to sixteen, it doesn't matter.

2. Across the board, and immediately, double the salary of every public school teacher K–12. Except in the case of middle school teachers, grades six to eight: triple their salaries.

3. Use the current teaching pool to mentor the new crop of teachers that my plan requires. Let us also offer experienced teachers yearlong sabbaticals every five years, for professional development and to forestall burnout.

4. Build the required classrooms, and make all classrooms, new and existing, adhere to these specifications: They must be cool in the summer, warm in the winter; they must be overfilled with "educational materials," including art and music and science supplies; they must be surrounded by vast playing fields. Spend far too much tax money on physical improvements.

5. Ensure that each student is fed both breakfast and lunch every single school day.

6. Ensure plenty of time for each student to stare out the window.
7. Abolish bake sales.

Let me return to point 1, the keystone of my plan. If you think the problems in our schools—unruly and violent behavior, astonishing dropout rates, bullying, academic failure, you name it—are not related to class size, you have not been in a classroom lately. The difference between teaching a class of thirty-six students and a class of eighteen students is profound. A teacher's job is not to corral students. A teacher needs to be able to see her students, know them, talk to them, teach them *how* to think: it is why we have school in the first place. If the classrooms of my youth had been twice as crowded, I might never have been able to find the teachers I did, those mentors, those guides, who ultimately saved me.

We must have more teachers, and everywhere, not only in the classroom, but in the halls and lunchrooms, and on the playgrounds.

School is not a factory that can be made more efficient by trimming employees and further mechanization; school is not a corporation, not a business. School is a human enterprise, and it is only made more efficient and effective when there are more teachers in the classrooms. Because that is where school happens, in the classroom.

More teachers now.

Mine is a simple proposal, and foolproof. An added benefit to my proposal is the creation of scads of new jobs, in the construction and educational supply sectors, surely, and for a highly paid and well-respected corps of teachers. I'm perfectly serious.

And to prove my seriousness, let me be the one to say it first. You may read my lips:

Raise my taxes!

Even though my daughter will go to a private high school, even though there will be much inefficiency in the implementation of my proposal, raise my taxes. Guarantee me that these new taxes will only go to the classroom—meaning to teachers and students directly—you can raise my taxes through the roof. Yes, raise them to Swedish levels, to "socialist" levels.

The bounty and luxury that were my public education were very expensive. And they were worth every penny.

Acknowledgments

I would like to thank the following for their time and expertise, and their devotion to their arts:

Meredith Eliassen, the Archer Collection of Historic Children's Materials at San Francisco State University

Kathy Kimpel, principal of Bagby Elementary School

Michael Posey, vice-principal of Branham High School

Keegan White and the students of Willow Grove School

Thomas Seaton, teacher and poet, of James Logan High School

The amazing Gary Bacon and the Learning Community of Los Altos/Mountain View High School, who allowed me to visit them for ten years

Barbara Alexander and the teachers of the Belvedere Montessori Preschool

The teachers and administration of the French American International School, San Francisco

The teachers and administration of the San Francisco Friends School

I must also thank ACME Studio, whose material sponsorship of my work has been such a pleasure. The longhand drafts of *Blackboard* were written with their "QWERTY" rollerball pen.

Lewis Buzbee is the author of *The Yellow-Lighted Bookshop*, *After the Gold Rush*, and *Fliegelman's Desire*, as well as three award-winning novels for younger readers, *Steinbeck's Ghost*, *The Haunting of Charles Dickens*, and *Bridge of Time*. He lives in San Francisco with his wife and daughter.

Book design by Ann Sudmeier. Composition by BookMobile Design & Digital Publisher Services, Minneapolis, Minnesota. Manufactured by Edwards Brothers Malloy on acid-free, 100 percent post-consumer wastepaper.